Kaleidoscope

Also by Patsy Clairmont

I Second That Emotion: Untangling Our Zany Feelings

Dancing Bones: Living Lively in the Valley

All Cracked Up: Experiencing God in the Broken Places

I Grew Up Little: Finding Hope in a Big God

The Hat Box: Putting on the Mind of Christ

The Shoe Box: Walking in the Spirit

I Love Being a Woman

*5 Cheesy Stories: About Friendship, Bravery,
Bullying and More*

Kaleidoscope

Seeing God's Wit and Wisdom in a Whole New Light

PATSY CLAIRMONT

THOMAS NELSON
Since 1798

NASHVILLE DALLAS MEXICO CITY RIO DE JANEIRO

Published in Nashville, Tennessee, by Thomas Nelson. Thomas Nelson is a registered trademark of Thomas Nelson, Inc.

Published in association with Books & Such Literary Agency, Janet Kobobel Grant, 52 Mission Circle, Suite 122, PMB 170, Santa Rosa, CA 95409

Thomas Nelson, Inc. titles may be purchased in bulk for educational, business, fund-raising, or sales promotional use. For information, please e-mail SpecialMarkets@ThomasNelson.com.

Unless otherwise noted, Scripture quotations are taken from the New King James Version®. © 1982 by Thomas Nelson, Inc. Used by permission. All rights reserved.

The Scripture quotation from *The Message* Bible is taken from *The Message* by Eugene H. Peterson. © 1993, 1994, 1995, 1996, 2000, 2001, 2002. Used by permission of NavPress Publishing Group. All rights reserved.

Library of Congress Cataloging-in-Publication Data

Clairmont, Patsy.
  Kaleidoscope : seeing God's wit and wisdom in a whole new light / Patsy Clairmont.
    p. cm.
  ISBN 978-1-4002-0270-6 (hardcover)
  1. Bible. O.T. Proverbs—Criticism, interpretation, etc. 2. Christian women—Religious life.
I. Title.
  BS1465.52.C53 2009
  248.8'43—dc22   2009045285

Printed in the United States of America

10 11 12 13 14 QG 9 8 7

To the Pink Sneaker Sisters . . . Ellie, Jan,
Anita, Kathy, Carol, Babbie, and Priscilla.
You girls add such color to the world!

Contents

CHAPTER 1

The Tube of Mirrors

The other day I stepped into a whimsical toy store . . . alone. Yes, I confess I'm just a kid disguised as an ancient artifact. I use the excuse that I'm a nana to peruse the playful offerings, when really I'm fascinated by the cleverness of so many of the designs. Who thinks these things up?

For instance, I saw a paunchy mouse. When you cranked its curly tail, it spit plastic cheese. Now, please, who wouldn't want one of those? Or what about the sinister talking dinosaur who threatened to eat your mother? Excuse me? Obviously the creator hadn't worked through his issues! Or my favorite, the calico cat that purred lullabies over her babies. Aw.

I started down an aisle, when my attention was drawn to a girl who looked to be about seven years old, standing near a display of puffy, pink kangaroos. She had just unearthed from a basket of action figures a kaleidoscope. It was a small one without much outer appeal, but she evidently was experienced with kaleidoscopes and seemed excited to investigate the surprise within it. First, she surveyed the cylinder from both ends; then she shook it; finally she pulled it up to her face as she turned toward the light. Her little face scrunched up in absolute focus as she rotated the tumbler and drank in the sights.

When she finished her visual tour, she set aside the kaleidoscope, which is when I inched my way toward it. I don't know if you're like this, but if someone sees something I can't see, I'm willing to pay extra for the view. Subtle as a semi in my attempt to reach the cardboard tube, I stumbled over a wagon full of iridescent sea lions. I'm grateful that the girl's attention was pinned to a bin of rubber lizards and light-up snakes, which gave me the opportunity to casually pick up the petite kaleidoscope and have a look-see for myself. And no, I didn't have to scrunch up my face to focus; mine came that way.

What is there about a kaleidoscope that tilts our world? I mean, who knew that a simple tube of mirrors filled with beads or pebbles that catch light and make geometric designs could captivate so many for so long? And yet they have. If you're like most of the population, you find it hard to pass one by on a store shelf without at least, like me, taking a quick peek. Probably because we know that, with one spin of the tumbler, we will see dynamic patterns transform again and again, creating our own art gallery that we help design by our touch. I'm sure our involvement is part of the draw, knowing that with each additional turn the view is new and mesmerizing, like a rainbow refracted in ocean waves lapping across white sands.

Every child delights in a visual roll through the world of wonder, but the enjoyment doesn't stop in childhood. I'm proof. I remain fascinated with the explosive color show twirling about inside a cylinder that offers me a private viewing of my own hand-held universe. It is no wonder to me that we adults meticulously design, fervently collect, artistically display, and passionately sell kaleidoscopes of all intricacies and sizes.

In fact, the largest one is circling in space over us at this very moment: the Hubble "kaleidoscope" captures the panoramic patterns of the heavens and tumbles them back to Earth. Through it we can explore the cascading bits and pieces of the universe via its eye and witness the most dangerous, spectacular, and mysterious depths of the cosmos.

The most expensive "earthly" kaleidoscope recorded was sold in 1987 by London's auction house, Sotheby's, for $75,000. (My husband and I bought our first home for only $21,000.) It is a brass cylinder mounted on a tripod and inscribed with these lines:

- Who could from thy outward case, half thy hidden beauties trace?
- Who from such exterior show, guess the gems within that glow!
- Emblem of the mind divine, cased within its mortal shrine.

The word *kaleidoscope* means "beautiful shapes to look at and examine." I think my favorite feature of kaleidoscopes, though, regardless of their beauty or collectibility, is their eclectic potential. Probably because, quite honestly, I'm an eclectic person. I dress as though I have tumbled out of a color wheel; I decorate my home in mixes of styles and hues; I like to cook without rhyme or reason. (My hubby refers to me and my in-kitchen escapades as "she who experiments.") My propensity for such diversity probably explains why I'm drawn to not only the fragmented somersaults within a kaleidoscope but also to the varied flurry of the book of Proverbs.

Proverbs is like a four-mirrored kaleidoscope that gives a parade of images. On first glance, this book appears to be an unorganized shopping list for a myriad of professions: parents, counselors, teachers, singles, wives—why, there is even a list of verses cautioning one from becoming a full-time, card-carrying fool. But in truth the parade of topics helps us see reflections of divine yet practical insights for daily living, regardless of profession.

What I personally find helpful when I twirl the proverbial cylinder are the verses on "mouth" that I often need to roll around in my head before my words spill out all over someone. For instance . . .

There is one who speaks like the piercings of a sword, but the tongue of the wise promotes health. (Proverbs 12:18)

Ouch! Are your words cutting-edge? When you slice through to the bottom line of an issue, is it at the expense of someone's feelings? I know I'm guilty. I'm thankful that, in this comparison, we are reminded that we have a choice, that our words can have life-giving potential.

Recently, a new friend on my Facebook page dropped me a note. In it she shared that she was a teacher and a cancer patient. As an educator, she had successfully used word boards in her classroom to teach a subject, so after her diagnosis she decided to start a word board for herself. This one would hang on the wall at the foot of her bed and be filled with words that nurtured and encouraged. On awakening, she would see those uplifting words.

I loved her idea and then had one of my own. I put out a request to my Facebook friends to send a word that they felt would add light and life to her project. It would be our way of helping to jump-start her get-well card for herself. A couple hundred women did just that. Life-giving words that promoted health poured in: *held, grace, wings, overcomer, belonging, chocolate, balm, hallelujah, safe, release, nurtured, refuge*, and *steadfast* were among the sweet words offered.

When, as a young adult, I first cried out to Christ to rescue and forgive me, I soon after recognized my need to study the words in the Bible. Life-giving words tumbled out: *peace, prayer, power*, and *provision*, among others. I was a desperate woman with a tumblerful of brokenness and not enough light to know what to do with it. So I did a lot of word studies in the light-bearing Scriptures during those emotionally spinning years as I searched for steadying answers. Initially my study style was splintered at best, but because of God's heart for His seeking children, He helped this wobbly lamb find pasture in His stabilizing Word.

It took me years of grazing to realize God's Word was its own commentary. The more I read and studied, the more I saw how one portion (bit) of Scripture was defining other portions (pieces). I found that exciting. That isn't to say I'm not aware of the benefits of researching what others have learned through their lifetimes of education and efforts in biblical studies. I'm a fan of Spurgeon, Chambers, Moody, et al.

One of the things I found so appealing about Proverbs was how direct it was. I didn't have to struggle to get it. Proverbs is an in-your-face kind of book. No easing you into truth, but bottom line, there it is—truth in its barest form:

He who hates correction is stupid. (Proverbs 12:1*b*)

See what I mean? No easy way to hide from that tumble with truth. Or how about . . .

He who trusts in his own heart is a fool. (Proverbs 28:26*a*)

Nope, I don't need to search through commentaries, wondering what those verses are trying to say. One twirl of the Proverbs cylinder and I get the gist.

I've struggled most of my life with a fragile emotional makeup. I identify with all those broken bits getting tossed around inside of kaleidoscopes. The inner repairs on the bits and pieces in my life have been ongoing, and I imagine that will continue until I dispose of this clunky earth suit and step through the veil. I'm almost certain my new suit will be svelte and won't jiggle when I walk. Until then I continue to search God's Word and hide it in my heart.

I'm not a Bible scholar; I don't know Greek or Hebrew. In fact, sometimes I make up words that don't even exist—you'll note that from time to time as you read. And don't squeal on me, but I can even forget to read my daily devotional. Yet here is what I know for sure: my heart has been changed through the straightforward counsel of Proverbs. And that is what these kaleidoscopic readings are about.

If you would like to join another lamb in search of good pasture, please come graze with me on the hillside of His love.

I hope you find the joy of these colorful verses with their direct wisdom, clear understanding, and their snappy offering of divine instruction. I will approach them in a hither-and-yon way, rather than numerically, staying with the kaleidoscopic design of spin and view. The questions at the end of each chapter, in the "Bits and Pieces" sections, are meant to help you personalize each chapter's opening proverb for yourself or within a group. The verses that follow, in the "Held to the Light" sections, support the chapter's topic, and when read in conjunction with the devotional thoughts, can add additional dynamics.

I pray that Christ will give you a heart full of wisdom to face the choices that come at you daily. Life is textured. May we be sturdy people, up to the task of living with joyful integrity.

So together let's survey some verses from both ends, give them a shake, and pull them up to our faces as we turn toward the light. Then we'll scrunch up our focus and drink in the sight. Whether you choose to spin the Proverbs tumbler alone or with a kaleidoscope of friends who gather together to capture patterns of God's ways for their lives, the result will be spectacular art!

CHAPTER 2

Weighty Matters

Do not boast about tomorrow, for you do not know what a day may bring forth.

—PROVERBS 27:1

The day had come for me to address the weight I had added on after an indulgent year of culinary delights—the Dairy Queen, to be specific. It might have been the way the scale groaned when I stepped on it that alerted me, or the mocking numbers that shuffled up to the arrow and spelled out "tractor-trailer," but this was the day. My goal: lose twenty pounds.

I thrust myself into a new regimen. Exercise began early in the day on my treadmill, followed by a fruit smoothie for breakfast and enough water to moisten the Sahara. Lunch was a sawdust disk using the alias of *rice cake*. I smeared it with peanut butter and decked it with wafer-thin banana slices. Dinner was mostly fresh veggies, with a snack of no-salt, baked chips to close out the day. The number of chips consumed: six. Not seven, but six. Woo-hoo!

After a week and a half of this punishment, resulting in a two-pound weight loss, I was ready to tell other people what they ought to do to lose weight. No kidding. I was thinking, *exercise video, diet books, movie contract . . .* Give me a hint of success, a dab behind one ear, and I puff up like a member of the Tetraodontidae.

Who are they, you ask? (Please ask.) They are a family of fish that includes my personal favorite, the puffer fish.

You probably have seen this fish swim by on the National Geographic channel. He's a medium-sized fish that, in the presence of a threat, puffs up to make others think he's bigger than he is. A strategic intimidation? A scaredy-cat maneuver that gives him time to get away? A quick weight-gain scheme so his predators can't gobble him up? Or one more example in nature that reveals truth? Or perhaps all of the above?

We all have puffer tendencies. Oh, it might be for different reasons—hoity-toity about our kids; heady over grandchildren; snobby over a job promotion; snooty over a new home; haughty over a fully loaded, hot-shot vehicle; inflated over weight loss . . .

For me, my weight-loss puffer-moment didn't last long because I hadn't counted on what a day would bring. I mean, how could I have known that at a Women of Faith event Marilyn Meberg would announce from stage that she loved lemon meringue pie? And then that a generous attendee would buy said pie and have it sent to the green room? And how could I have predicted it would arrive at the lunch table just as I had completed a dry salad complemented by stale croutons?

There it sat, like a work of art, smack-dab in front of me. Mile-high, shiny meringue piled into peaks and lightly browned, settled over yellow, almost transparent, lemon filling that hugged the edges of a flaky crust. Then Marilyn, generous person that she is, announced, "Would anyone like some?"

To say I flung myself face-first into this sea of delight would be an overstatement. Almost. People stared as I quickly coaxed an enormous piece out of the pan and onto my plate.

Halfway through this extravagant encounter, a young man nearby inquired if it was good.

I replied with downcast eyes, "Don't bother; it's not worth the calories." I peeked up and noticed his eyebrows suspiciously arched into his knit cap. Minutes passed, and the invasive fellow pointed out that for someone who was unimpressed with the offering, I had done everything but lick the platter. *Harrumph.*

That pie incident slung open the swinging doors of my appetite, and over the next four weeks, I ate wildly. I not only found the two pounds I had lost, but I also gained three more.

Do not boast . . .

Seems simple enough. Three little words. They aren't even big words until you try to live them. Do we not understand? Oh, we might not like the parental tone of it, but we aren't confused by "don't do it!" So it must be the *boast* that trips us.

Boast: to speak with excessive pride, to brag, to crow, to swagger, to gloat, to exaggerate.

Boasting is interesting because we can detect it in a hot minute in another person, and I can safely say, it's usually off-putting unless, of course, you have two puffer fish attempting to outpuff each other. Then it's downright nauseating. Yet that same quality isn't as easy to pinpoint in our own behavior. It tends to dive down into our ego to gloat.

Of course, we live in a time when swagger and gloat are lauded. One week on *American Idol*, Simon Cowell announced to one of the young contestants that he should be "done with humility." Cowell's statement suggested that an inflated ego would make the guy better star material. *Hmm.*

The theory that only the swagger-filled confident people succeed seems rampant in our society. It's a puffer-fish theology of "fake it until you make it." But here's the problem: We don't have a clue about what tomorrow might bring. Tomorrow is already full, but we didn't pack it.

It reminds me of a trip my hubby and I took years ago.

Actually, Les was a stunned participant on this particular adventure. I kidnapped him from his job, and I had packed a suitcase for him that awaited in the car's trunk. Everything in his luggage was new and unknown to him; so when we arrived at our destination, he was surprised by the case's contents. He couldn't have guessed beyond a general theme what was inside. The details were revealed upon the arrival.

The same is true for us. We don't know until a day is unpacked how it will look. None of us could have foreseen the tragedy of 9/11, or that a fierce storm could hit our rich country and that we would not immediately be there for the victims, or that our investments would be wiped out, or that banks would close, or that young people across our land would riddle their classmates with revenge. Who knew? Not us.

Only puffer fish can exaggerate their size without consequences. The rest of us need to take heed, as *The Message* Bible states, "Don't brashly announce what you're going to do tomorrow; you don't know the first thing about tomorrow" (Proverbs 27:1).

Bits and Pieces

1. What was the last thing you were determined to do that fizzled?
2. To whom had you boasted about your plan?
3. What puffer-fish people do you know?
4. What traits do they display that you find off-putting?
5. Define humility.
6. If you could pack "tomorrow," what would you put in it?
7. What has life taught you about tomorrow?

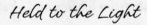

Held to the Light

For the wicked boasts of his heart's desire; he blesses the greedy and renounces the LORD. (Psalm 10:3)

Those who trust in their wealth and boast in the multitude of their riches, none of them can by any means redeem his brother, nor give to God a ransom for him. (Psalm 49:6–7)

But now you boast in your arrogance. All such boasting is evil. (James 4:16)

My soul shall make its boast in the LORD; the humble shall hear of it and be glad. (Psalm 34:2)

CHAPTER 3

Custom Fit

A word fitly spoken . . .

—PROVERBS 25:11*a*

I like things that fit. Yet that almost never happens for me without the intervention of a seamstress or tailor, which is one of the challenges of being 4'12" in stature. Usually my slacks, even in petite lengths, have enough extra fabric trailing off my feet that I could, with the remnants, reupholster an overstuffed chair and matching ottoman. It frustrates me that much of the added embellishments and flair are on the part that's cut off and pitched, which plays havoc with the original design and decreases the value of my investment. Yes, I have learned to appreciate a good fit.

As we'll see in a moment, this proverb suggests that God puts a high price tag on fit as well. The fit mentioned, though, isn't about length, pattern, design, or fashion but, instead, is about spoken words.

Actually, on second thought, words can be like a fitted garment because when they have been measured out in such a way that they hang correctly on the recipient, when they have been fashioned from the heart and designed to add value, they become a priceless addition to the wardrobe of others.

Speaking of hanging correctly, have you ever noticed what a physical and emotional relief it is finally to have the muddle in our brains deciphered, our thoughts shaken out and hung up in a tidy manner? Out of sheer gratitude, we want to reward the one who purposely or inadvertently gave us the gift of a tailored expression. It's as if that person knew our measurements (eek!) and altered the conversation just for us.

That happened for Jennifer, when she realized she had

made a serious error that involved two of her clients. The mistake would mean a significant financial loss for each person. At first, Jennifer thought about just pretending she hadn't noticed the error. Or maybe she could dress up the mistake so it looked as if it were someone else's. But finally she chose to own up and to take responsibility.

The first client she called was cool but civil. Jennifer figured it was hard to ask for more, in light of the damage she had caused.

When she told Ann, her second client, the phone line went silent for a bit. Then as Jennifer held her breath, Ann said, "Thank God, you're human!" Ann went on to say that Jennifer had performed at such a high level for so long, it was a relief to discover she could make errors. Talk about words of gold and silver! Ann's kindness gave Jennifer room to forgive herself and brought her sweet release from guilt.

We all have had words said to us that captured our attention and caused our ears to perk up because they just, well, fit our situation. We wonder how they knew. Perhaps they expressed what we longed to hear, as happened for Jennifer. Or they put into words what we had been feeling but hadn't been able to articulate. When we heard them say the words aloud, we thought, *That's it; that's how I feel.* We know that we have experienced a eureka moment, when we have struck a rich vein, the dazzling gold and silver of truth.

. . . is like . . . (Proverbs 25:11*b*)

How many times in an attempt to describe something to someone have you tried to define the item by comparing it to something you and the listener both knew? Perhaps you were describing a color: "The orange *is like* pumpkins in the fall." Or you might explain how the mother of the neighbor children is like a roaring lion. Or you might emphasize that the latest jab from your mother-in-law is like . . . well, never mind. You get the idea.

The "proverbist" (yes, I made up that word) used *is like* to help us grasp the value attached to a well-placed word as well as to enlarge our definition. *Is like* is a window to help us gain a clearer view. *Is like* helps us see what we are hearing. *Is like* is morning sunlight filling a shadowed corner.

So here it comes . . . "A word fitly spoken is like . . ."

. . . apples of gold in settings of silver. (Proverbs 25:11*c*)

What a picturesque scene that paints! Just imagine for a moment that you enter a room and see a splendid, golden gleam and a sterling glimmer, only to find out that the golden apples and silver settings are yours. All yours; you get to take them home.

A couple of years ago I had the delight of having dinner in the home of a well-known personality. I felt like a scullery maid who had slipped in undetected to dine with the queen's court. When we arrived, her dining room had been transformed into an elegant French café, with multiple tables draped in floor-length tablecloths, the chairs bedecked in fabric and tulle, and stupendous arrangements centered on each table. The multi-layered china, sparkling goblets, and gleaming silver settings took my breath away. At each person's seat was a six-inch gold cross with pearl insets that was our gift to take home. As you can imagine we, her guests, were thrilled.

What a memorable keepsake. It represented far more than a dinner present and has been a reminder not only of her generosity but also of her well-designed party full of warmth and words . . . words chosen to honor her guests, to make even scullery maids feel welcome.

We have the opportunity daily to consider the guests who enter our circle of influence—the gal at the cash register, the man at the post office, the kid in our flower beds, the neighbor in our business, the teen in our faces.

We can fashion words to fit each heart that will be easy for the recipient to receive, something that will remain with him or her and continue to build equanimity. We can care for others by using words that gleam with love, that sparkle with authenticity, and that shimmer long after the conversation is over. Most important, we can choose words that fit each person perfectly. I can't think of a better way for us to share the cross of Christ than in a conversation full of divinely appointed words that are spoken at the precise moment they need to be said.

Yes, I appreciate a good fit.

Bits and Pieces

1. When was the last time your brain felt muddled? Did anyone help you decipher your feelings? What did that person say?
2. Can you describe how you are feeling right now with an "is like" statement (e.g., How I feel is like a fish out of water)?
3. When was the last time you felt that you spoke words that fit the recipient? How did that make you feel?

4. Thumb through a dictionary and find five golden words that are full of life (e.g., *sagacious, charismatic, hearten*). Ask God to help you correctly fit them into your conversations with others.
5. Start a Golden Word collection—fresh, life-giving words that aren't part of your daily conversation but that make people feel valued. Write them on index cards or carry a small notepad until they are natural for you to use.

Held to the Light

Your words have upheld him who was stumbling, and you have strengthened the feeble knees. (Job 4:4)

Words of the wise, spoken quietly, should be heard rather than the shout of a ruler of fools. (Ecclesiastes 9:17)

The words of a wise man's mouth are gracious, but the lips of a fool shall swallow him up. (Ecclesiastes 10:12)

If you abide in Me, and My words abide in you, you will ask what you desire, and it shall be done for you. (John 15:7)

CHAPTER 4

Heavy Lifting

*The way of the L*ORD *is strength for the upright.*

—PROVERBS 10:29*a*

What do you need strength to do? Strength to face a calamity, face an enemy, face a deadline, face a health issue, or maybe just face tomorrow? Here's a biggie for me . . . face myself!

My calendar is thinning by sheer odds. I'm grateful my days are appointed by the Lord and not assigned by statistics or even diagnosis. Yet I'm aware that I have fewer days left than I have used already. Somehow I went from being young to, now, not so much. And my birthdays seem to be on spin cycle; I'm surprised that, at the rate they are being slung at me, the icing stays on my cakes.

I recently read that the great radio personality Paul Harvey was offered the largest salary of any radio broadcaster in history at the age of eighty-two. Woo-hoo! Ten million dollars a year made him a national treasure . . . right? Nope. What made him of such value for so long was that God had strengthened him for his assigned task, and Paul had walked upright in fulfilling it until his death in 2009. He and his wife were vocal about faith being their source of strength.

I'm cheered on by Harvey's viability since I, too, would like to stay mentally aligned and physically upright for as long as possible. Here's my concern . . . leakage. Brain cell seepage. I'm, at times, mentally suspect . . . even to myself.

These days I'm carrying a large, shiny, bright orange-yellow purse, which can be seen from Detroit to Dallas and takes considerable strength to lift. I call her Bertha. She stands at approximately one-third of my height, which when she's slung over my shoulder, can give the appearance that I'm leaning toward Georgia. I've always loved the South.

Because of all my travel back and forth across our nation, I have occasion to need many different items, which I have tucked hither and yon into the folds of Bertha's belly. While I know I've placed them in there, when I actually need an item, finding it becomes a geographical struggle, as well as a mental health issue.

This is how it usually plays out: I dig around in search of, say, my cell phone, only to bump into every other item but the phone. I then become mildly irritated and begin a more intense examination of the purse's interior, unzipping pockets and pouches, with intermittent stirring of items. I reach down into the lower peninsula of the purse and feel every possession as if I'm reading Braille. Then in frustration, I stick my whole head inside in hopes of spotting the renegade phone. When that fails, I pull on the purse straps as if they were the Jaws of Life while dragging the bigger items out into the open. Finally, fully miffed, I vigorously dump the entire contents onto the airport seat next to me, watching the overflow actually over-flow—tissues, my husband's clunky car keys (what are they doing in there?), hand sanitizer, half-eaten candy bars, and gum wrappers float and clatter to the floor.

Then, thinking I might have dropped my phone into my briefcase, I dump its contents on the surrounding floor: computer, Kindle, Bible, cords, chargers, file folders, socks, magazines, glasses . . .

I'm aware I'm being watched by nearby passengers waiting to board our flight. Men look stumped as to how and why anyone would have that much debris. Women pay little mind to my struggle but, instead, give me that T-shirt look of *been there, done that*. Well, except for those arched-eyebrow ones who are carrying a handbag the size of a pea pod. Whereas, wide-eyed children sidle over to see if they can find something fun, mistaking my paraphernalia for the Dollar Store, teenagers look embarrassed and disgusted at the old lady and her piles of junk.

Then as I stare down at all my personal litter, I have a revelation . . . I no longer have any idea what I'm searching for. Zip. Nada.

It's usually at this juncture that two things happen: (1) the announcement comes over the intercom that the flight is now boarding; and (2) my phone rings from the safety of my jacket pocket. It's my hubby wondering if I know what happened to his car keys.

By the time I jam everything back in my bags, board the plane, find my seat, and crush my bulging carry-ons under the seat in front of me, I'm full of self-disgust. It probably doesn't help that I'm seated next to the gal who has her pea pod sitting on her lap with a smug smile across her tidy little face. I bet she knows exactly where her cell phone is—and every brain cell, for that matter.

That's why I need strength to face myself. Well, at least it's one of the reasons. There's more. Nope, I'm not telling; I'll leave you to imagine. Just remember this: a woman at any age who is weighed down by her overstuffed bags has trouble walking upright . . . and remains exhausted.

What taxes your strength?

Bits and Pieces

1. What is hard for you to face?
2. How's your calendar stacking up?
3. What are you carrying these days?
4. What weighs on your mental health?
5. When was the last time you forgot what you were looking for?
6. What is it that you find hard to keep track of?
7. How would you describe what self-disgust feels like?
8. What's inside your "bags"?
9. What robs you of your strength?

Held to the Light

Come to Me, all you who labor and are heavy laden, and I will give you rest. Take My yoke upon you and learn from Me, for I am gentle and lowly in heart, and you will find rest for your souls. For my yoke is easy and my burden is light. (Matthew 11:28–30)

So teach us to number our days, that we may gain a heart of wisdom. (Psalm 90:12)

My grace is sufficient for you, for My strength is made perfect in weakness. (2 Corinthians 12:9a)

> For the LORD is righteous, He loves righteousness; His countenance beholds the upright. *(Psalm 11:7)*

> The LORD is the strength of my life. *(Psalm 27:1b)*

CHAPTER 5

Babbling

He who has knowledge spares his words.

—PROVERBS 17:27*a*

Uh-oh. Right off the bat I know I'm in over my head, vowels and verbs up to my eyebrows, when it comes to this proverb. I'd like to think I'm knowledgeable, but if the criterion is using words sparingly, then I'm going to have to reevaluate.

I mean, sometimes I'm quiet. Actually, very quiet. And I've learned to be a listener. But I would have to confess that after I've been quiet for a while and listened for a spell, I've been known to burst into babble. It's not all babble—as in nonsensical—because I have some good stuff to say, but when I repeat what I've said or go into unnecessary details—and I do mean unnecessary—I'm downright "babbly."

I love words. Always have. They are powerful, important, influential, endearing, instructive, inspiring, and tender. But like a kaleidoscope when the cylinder is spun in the shadows and we see a dark and different design, so, too, words have the tainted potential to be devastating, defeating, derogatory, discriminating, demeaning, and divisive.

Notice this proverb doesn't say knowledge is silent but rather suggests that knowledge is into selectivity and brevity. This brings to mind a picture of an old man leaning on the steady cane of knowledge; attached to his belt is a small purse. Inside that purse reside his carefully chosen words for the day. He has counted them out, and he holds them close until needed. Note the contrast in size and purpose between the cane and the purse.

I know from experience that the longer I talk, the more

likely I am to regret something I say. *Hmm*. Maybe that's what this verse is about. You think?

Tell that to the prince . . .

Once upon a time there was a prince who, through no fault of his own, was cast under a spell by an evil witch. The curse was that the prince could speak only one word each year. However, he could save up the words so that if he didn't speak for a whole year, the following year he was allowed to speak two words.

One day he met a beautiful princess (ruby lips, golden hair, sapphire eyes) and fell madly in love. With the greatest difficulty, he decided to refrain from speaking for two whole years so he could look at her and say, "My darling." But at the end of the two years, he wished to tell her that he loved her. Because of this, he waited three more years without speaking, bringing his silence to a total of five years.

But at the end of the five years, he realized that he had to ask her to marry him. So he waited *another* four years without speaking.

Finally, as the ninth year of silence ended, his joy knew no bounds. Leading the lovely princess to the most secluded and romantic place in the beautiful royal garden, the prince heaped a hundred red roses on her lap, knelt before her, and taking her hand in his, said huskily, "My darling, I love you! Will you marry me?"

The princess tucked a strand of golden hair behind a dainty ear, opened her sapphire eyes in wonder, and parting her ruby lips, said, "Pardon?"

I'm grateful we aren't being asked to limit our words to one per year but, instead, to allow knowledge to support our existence, accessorized by our wisely filled purse.

... and a man of understanding is of a calm spirit. (Proverbs 17:27*b*)

I'm drawn to calm people. Not vacant, like the light is on, but nobody's home. Not arrogant, as if they're holding tight to the reins of control. I'm drawn, instead, to those who exude "settledness," a centeredness. Their insides aren't churning. Their tongues aren't wagging. They aren't fretting, stewing, or clamoring. They are functioning in their gifts and aren't threatened by yours. They are anchored in Christ, and the sea within them is still. I find that kind of steadiness compelling.

Calm isn't innately who I am. My insides have always been skittish, which I'm sure is why I'm drawn to soft music, gentle rain, and quiet spaces. I need the soothing influence they offer.

Some time ago, a friend who hadn't seen me for a couple of years commented that I was much quieter on my insides than she had known me to be in the past. "That's the only way I know how to say what I'm feeling and experiencing, Patsy," she said sweetly after a lengthy visit.

I remember being so heartened by her assessment because I felt that God was confirming the work He was doing in me. Like sparks from a flint when they catch soft kindling, the flame of Christ's presence and the work of His Spirit were being seen in my life. I was thrilled.

While I've continued to calm down through the years— thanks to Christ's promise that the work He begins within us He will complete—my tendency still is to be inwardly jiggly. The evidence of that came two years ago when I received an unexpected invitation to have both a colonoscopy and an endoscopy as part of the getting-older health regime.

To my surprise the tests revealed stomach ulcers. Stomachaches were a regular part of my life, but I wasn't prepared to hear I had ulcers. I believe that might be referred to as denial.

Ulcers are so, uh, well, unspiritual. At first I decided they were the kind caused by a virus, and I could pop a pill and skip on, but the doctor quickly ruled that out, saying mine weren't that kind. They were more the homegrown variety. Instead of an easy remedy, the doc gave me a list of dos and don'ts. Oh, great!

I, of course, had to change my diet, add light exercise to help with tension, and learn to deal with life pressures more calmly. May I say it has been easier to leave tomatoes off my plate and add a short walk to my routine than it has been to digest life differently. And leaving off tomatoes but adding walks is no easy task—in fact, it's an ongoing battle for me. Why, I could eat a tub—that would be a bathtub—of salsa before bedtime, and walks seem so, well, boring to me. I want to thunder, as in a Harley, not sashay down the boulevard. My mental idle revs high.

While I have come a long way from the anxiety-ridden days of my agoraphobia, obviously I have an even longer way to go to reach the shore of calm. One of the things I realized I would have to do was forgive myself for having this health condition. I thought I had walked with Christ too long to be toting around ulcers. What kind of testimony was that? How could I tell others that Christ was the Prince of Peace and then confess that my insides were riddled with sores?

I also had to forgive my dad. He, too, battled stomach ulcers that plagued him most of his adult life, and I thought, when I heard the doctor's diagnosis, *Thanks, Dad. One more thing you gave me that I didn't want.*

I know my response was unreasonable because certainly Dad never planned on handing down a propensity to develop ulcers, but that's where I was, and I had to deal with it from there.

Understanding often comes as we wade through our own thinking. In doing so (again), I discovered *new* insights in my old thoughts that were keeping me from the deeper calm I desired.

For instance, I'm trying to own that I'm way too hard on myself. For years my friends have told me, almost in unison, that I'm too "cranky" with me. I have deflected those comments, not sure what I was supposed to do about it. My expectations, for myself and at times for others, have angelic dust on them because I set them so high. Perfectionism, I know, is a strict taskmaster who offers no free lunches, much less recess.

We will always be less than we hoped at some level until we stand before the only Perfect One. We live in a fallen world, where disease is rampant and imperfections are the rule of the day but where Christ, who understands our frailty, makes provision for us. If we can grasp that, we will not be as wobbly, calm will keep us sane, and we will become like Jesus.

But when? Just beyond the veil of time when we come into completion.

Understanding that eternity is where and when Jesus finishes up His work within us definitely calms me. I thought I needed to be fixed before I got there, so I kept dragging myself into the workshop, tightening the vise, and hammering away. Here's the truth: I don't have to strive. Jesus has things under divine control.

Until that day when Jesus makes all things new, may we

together continue to forgive ourselves, forgive others, and let go, not of worthy goals, but of perfectionism.

Here are a few ways I've found that help me do that:

- I bless, in Christ's name, my day's journey. This helps me to move consciously through my day with calmer purpose.
- I speak aloud truth to my body by quoting Scripture that nurtures the life of Christ within me.
- I exercise gratitude, which keeps my heart supple and lessens my inner churning.

Oh, yes, and I'm trying, yes, trying, to eat right and to walk regularly.

Is it working? Truthfully, I'm sporadic. I find I don't excel at "a long obedience in the same direction" (which is how author Eugene Peterson described the kind of obedience we all strive for but most fail in). So I have to recommit weekly and sometimes daily . . . want to join me?

Bits and Pieces

1. When was the last time you babbled?
2. How did you feel after your babble ran dry? Relieved? Guilty? Shallow?
3. How do you deal with something you said that you know you shouldn't have?
4. When have you said important words to someone who couldn't hear you? What have you done with the hurt that created?

5. Is calm a part of your MO? Would others agree?
6. Who do you need to forgive for something he or she couldn't help?
7. Do you need to forgive yourself? When will you do that?

Held to the Light

In the multitude of words sin is not lacking, but he who restrains his lips is wise. (Proverbs 10:19)

Do not be rash with your mouth, and let not your heart utter anything hastily before God. For God is in heaven, and you on earth; therefore let your words be few. (Ecclesiastes 5:2)

Receive, please, instruction from His mouth, and lay up His words in your heart. (Job 22:22)

My words come from my upright heart; my lips utter pure knowledge. (Job 33:3)

The words of the LORD are pure words, like silver tried in a furnace of earth, purified seven times. (Psalm 12:6)

How sweet are Your words to my taste, sweeter than honey to my mouth! (Psalm 119:103)

CHAPTER 6

Barnyard Wisdom

Be diligent to know the state of your flocks,
and attend to your herds.

—PROVERBS 27:23

If I were a goat, I'd want to belong to my friend Ruthann. She is the most devoted goat "herdess" (yes, herdess) I've known. Okay, okay, she's the *only* goat herdess I've ever met, but I recognize a good thing when I see it. This lady is committed to her animals, which, by the way, aren't limited to goats. She also has horses, chickens, and honeybees. Oh, yes, and a couple of cats.

When Ruthann's goats hear her voice, they become downright verbal or "goatal" (made it up). Goats Ruby, Ava, Heidi, Katy Scarlett, and Emma Lee know their caregiver. The other day I walked out to the barn to see Ruby and Ava, who let me know before I ever reached the fence, that they weren't happy to see me. Their goatal (yes, I said it again) sounds were filled with disapproval, and they frowned, which I wouldn't have realized until Ruthann joined me fence-side, and I watched glee spread across their hairy faces. Those girls did everything but click their hooves in delight just to have Ruthann near.

Animals require a lot of care, time, money, and protection from themselves as well as from predators. Sort of like us. Recently, just before sunrise, Ruthann heard loud goatal cries, as if the "girls" were in distress. Clad only in her nightshirt, thinking her herd in danger, Ruthann dashed out the front door into the dark morning and sprinted down the unlit path, not knowing the danger that lay ahead. She reached the barn only to discover the girls were in a spat that resolved itself by the time she made her breathless arrival.

Let me say it again: if I were a goat, park me in one of

Ruthann's stalls. Just back the pickup to her barn, and I'll gladly trot in. And may I add, if I had heard the night goat commotion, I would have alerted the goat police or the goat squad because I don't do dark. The thought of sprinting on an unlit path gives me the willies. Add a barn in the scenario, not to mention the mysterious ruckus, and as far as I'm concerned, you have a *CSI* episode. I need a flood of light, as in major kilowatts, for my hooves before I inch forward.

Some of us just aren't barn-ish. And you know who you are, so don't smirk at me. I believe, bottom line, this chapter's verse is saying, "Mind your own business." If you are a farmer, herdess, shepherd, receptionist, waitress, beautician, parent, executive, teacher, or whatever, tend to what has been entrusted to your care.

Did you know that if you don't water houseplants, they wither and die? Of course. I knew this, too, but I must have had one of those brain freezes a person experiences when she takes a mouthful of rocky road ice cream because, after receiving some lovely plants as gifts, I forgot. By the time my brain thawed, my plants were kissing the dirt. It was mine to care for them, but I hadn't tended to my job.

Did you know that if a teacher invests in an unruly child, she can change the direction of his or her life? Former president Jimmy Carter quoted his grade-school teacher in his inaugural address. Why? She had tended well to her flocks, and students do not soon forget. Many famous people credit their teachers for being the shepherds in their character formation and career decisions.

The word *diligent* used in this proverb is packed full of meaning. To be diligent is to esteem and to love. It's seen in one's behavior of steady, constant, earnest, dedicated, energetic, lively effort. *Diligent* also means to make well, to be skillful, to discern, to search for, and to be careful.

Also, to be diligent is to give attention to, to set your heart on something or someone. The phrase *attend to* is to know well the face of, as in appearance.

Most moms recognize at a glance when something is up with their herd. Years ago I remember walking through the living room and noticing a look on my toddler's face that stopped me in my tracks. He hadn't said a word, but I knew that precious little face. I had memorized every nook and cranny around his mouth, nose, and eyes since his birth, and something that day set off an alarm in my shepherdess's heart. I questioned him while scanning the surroundings, and that's when I spotted it . . . an empty bottle of baby aspirin that he had knocked down off a high shelf in the kitchen and consumed. Needless to say, nightshirt-emergency activity followed. I'm thankful that story ended well . . . because I knew my little lamb's face.

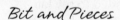

Bit and Pieces

1. If you were a farm animal, who would you want to be in charge of your care? Why?
2. Whom have you run in your nightshirt to rescue? What happened?
3. Have you ever arrived somewhere, excited to see someone, only to realize that he or she wasn't happy to see you? What have you done to "tend" to those feelings?
4. When, if ever, have you sprinted down a dark path?

5. Are you barn-ish?
6. What teacher has most affected your life? How?
7. In what ways are you diligent?
8. Whose appearance do you know well?
9. What have you been given to do?
10. In what ways do you tend your herd or flock?

Held to the Light

Watch therefore, and pray always that you may be counted worthy to escape all these things that will come to pass, and to stand before the Son of Man. (Luke 21:36)

Watch, stand fast in the faith, be brave, be strong. (1 Corinthians 16:13)

My sheep hear My voice, and I know them, and they follow Me. (John 10:27)

So he shepherded them according to the integrity of his heart, and guided them by the skillfulness of his hands. (Psalm 78:72)

CHAPTER 7

Cutting Edge

As iron sharpens iron, so a man sharpens
the countenance of his friend.

—PROVERBS 27:17

When you think of friends gathering together, what comes to mind—garden parties, lunch dates, Bible studies, or maybe scrapbooking retreats? What about knife-sharpening get-togethers? No? Really?

What does sharpening knives have to do with friendship? That thought seems way out in left field . . . that is, until we "hone in" on Proverbs 27:17.

Hone: to sharpen with a whetstone, to create a cutting edge as on knives and scissors, to make more focused and efficient.

If you've watched someone sharpen a knife, you know a lot of grinding goes on, which causes sparks to fly.

At first I wondered if this proverb were suggesting that we should grind on each other's nerves. I've been there and done that. Quite honestly, it didn't seem to help a whit.

Well, actually, I believe this verse is speaking of the kind of investments that help each person to become keener in her perceptions, sharper in her wit, and more directed in her energies.

In all honesty relationships haven't been easy for me, but I continue to work hard to learn. If I could offer you a foot-up in your relationships, it would be this truth that has taken years for me to get ahold of: "we can't give away what isn't ours."

Plain and simple: we know more than we live. And when we try to tell others what they ought to do, even if we're right, we won't ring true to our advice if we aren't living our own counsel. Authenticity is the cutting edge that adds relevancy to our offering.

If I know you've paid your dues to learn a truth, you better believe I'm going to lean into your experiential whetstone to sharpen my perspective. But if you're talking big yet living small, I won't be drawn to the tinkling brass of your verbal offering.

I've been blessed to have hundreds of honed women step through my life. These women are attempting to live their lives with a clear ring, and I've deeply benefited from their counsel.

Occasionally they tell me what I don't want to hear, but those who are walking their talk are hard to resist because I'm aware that their comments are neither frivolous nor untested. After integrating their insights into my life, now that I'm older than Methuselah's last haircut, my offerings to others are more beneficial.

The sharpest knives I own have sheaths to protect me from being cut when I reach into the drawer. Likewise, I've noted that individuals who have been through the steely rubbings of hardship are sheathed in empathy. Their intentions aren't meant to be cutting. They realize that truth's edge will be severe enough, and they need not bear down. They aren't confused; their experiences have taught them that they aren't the Holy Spirit. They offer us the keen truths they've learned, but God's Spirit alone forges our character.

Bits and Pieces

1. Who are the cutting-edge people in your life?
2. How have they sharpened your perspective?
3. Who helps you stay focused?

4. Who in your life demonstrates a winsome wit?

5. Is wit important to you? Why or why not?

6. Are you empathetic? Energetic?

7. How is God at work within you?

Held to the Light

Greater love has no one than this, than to lay down one's life for his friends. (John 15:13)

But God demonstrates His own love toward us, in that while we were still sinners, Christ died for us. (Romans 5:8)

Finally, all of you be of one mind, having compassion for one another; love as brothers, be tenderhearted, be courteous. (1 Peter 3:8)

Be kindly affectionate to one another with brotherly love, in honor giving preference to one another. (Romans 12:10)

CHAPTER 8

It's a Mad, Mad World

Like a madman who throws firebrands, arrows,
and death, is the man who deceives his neighbor,
and says, "I was only joking!"

—PROVERBS 26:18–19

A madman, simply put, is a man full of mad: imagine a glass pitcher of gasoline, full to the brim, which the slightest jiggle will cause to spill over. Now, when I say man, I'm not just referring to the male of the species but to humankind. We all need to check if our pots are seeping over with ire. You know a madman (or madwoman) by the way he hurls words that burn, puncture, and bring death . . .

Anger is only one letter short of danger. (Anonymous)

A madman is scary because he has stepped over a line, and we sense it. Sometimes he bellows to intimidate or to control. And sometimes he loses control and doesn't know how to step back into sanity's lines of safety . . .

Sometimes when I'm angry, I have the right to be angry, but that doesn't give me the right to be cruel. (Author unknown)

My husband's dad was often a drunken madman. In fact, his rage, like a tipped, scalding cauldron, spewed out over his six children and wife regularly. Theirs was a scary world of obscenities, beatings, and midnight ranting. The children never knew what might set off his scathing responses nor when. It wasn't unusual for the children to be jarred awake in the night to the muffled cries of their mother being beaten. It terrified them.

My mother-in-law left Les's dad, taking the children, many times, but once he sobered up, he would go after them and promise never to be that way again. His I-was-only-joking apologies left the family reeling with insecurities as they waited to see if they were truly safe. They were not.

Then one night Les's dad came staggering into the house out of a snowstorm, but this time he wasn't drunk. His odd behavior and nonsensical talk frightened the family, and they weren't certain what to make of it. Suddenly he fell into eye-rolling seizures. His sons, seeing he was incapacitated and couldn't hurt them, moved him to the car and rushed him to the hospital. Les and another brother were carrying their dad into the emergency room when he went limp in their arms. The madman had died . . . at the age of forty-six.

That wintry night while he had died, the wounds left by his firebrands, arrows, and death-breathing behavior swirled on in the taunting memories, tortured self-esteems, and tangled fears of his family. They would spend the rest of their lives sorting out the violent impact he had on them collectively and individually.

Many of us can't imagine that kind of brutality. Yet I know I've been guilty in an angry moment of hurling hurtful words and then in an attempt to avoid responsibility for my behavior have claimed, "I was only kidding." I wonder if that's the path— when we're unchecked and unconfessed—that eventually leads to becoming a madman. What a scary thought that we stagger so near the cliff of madness.

If we had a machine that could detect scars on our hearts, I wonder how many of the wounds would have been caused by a piercing arrow of jealousy, a firebrand of envy, or a deadly word of revenge—all forms of anger. If we aren't cautious, we will dress up these familiar emotions in the clothing of *our rights*. Then we believe we have a rationale for our behavior. That's a slippery slope to long-term madman status . . .

> Resentment is like taking poison and waiting for the other person to die. (Malachy McCourt)

I'm concerned for our society by the level of anger and brutality in our entertainment. Vile language seems to be a necessity to receive the ratings that draw folks to the box office. Audiences pay to hear madmen rage and violent language to be flung into the air, ripping holes in the viewers' dignity, numbing their sensitivities, and smudging their moral decency. The very thing that Les's family prayed to escape, people now crowd in to participate in. How sad.

And we wonder why violence and fear are escalating in our world . . .

> Anger blows out the lamp of the mind. (Robert G. Ingersoll)

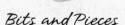

Bits and Pieces

1. Who do you know who would make it on a madman list?
2. In what ways does anger scare you?
3. Have you ever said, "I was only kidding"? Were you?
4. What have you spent a lifetime sorting out?
5. What fears cause you to knot up?

6. If you could guess, how many scars do you think are on your heart?
7. Who put them there?
8. How do jealousy, envy, and revenge touch your life?
9. How does brutal language affect you?

Held to the Light

Be strong and of good courage, do not fear nor be afraid of them; for the LORD your God, He is the One who goes with you. He will not leave you nor forsake you. (Deuteronomy 31:6).

I sought the LORD, and He heard me, and delivered me from all my fears. (Psalm 34:4)

Fear not, for I am with you; be not dismayed, for I am your God . . . Yes, I will help you, I will uphold you with My righteous hand. (Isaiah 41:10)

You shall fear the LORD your God and serve Him, and shall take oaths in His name. (Deuteronomy 6:13)

CHAPTER 9

Words du Jour

A man shall eat well by the fruit of his mouth.

—PROVERBS 13:2*a*

Have you ever considered that our spoken words not only go out, but they also go in? Yes, our words originate inside of us, but when spoken, they re-impact us. When we say something spiteful, we pay double. Our words rumble back in and traipse through our interiors, increasing our anxiety and decreasing our sense of harmony.

If our last conversation were translated into a lunch menu, would we look forward to ordering off of it? If we spoke sweetly, no problem, but if we were hostile, well, break out the Zantac!

Proverbs 13:2 promises that "a man shall eat well by the fruit of his mouth."

The first fruit that comes to my mind is found in Galatians 5:22–23, in which we're told "the fruit of the Spirit is love, joy, peace, longsuffering, kindness, goodness, faithfulness, gentleness, self-control."

Now, that's a lip-smacking menu!

Actually, I think if we used that list of fruit as filters, so that we pressed our words through goodness, gentleness, peace, etc., before speaking them, our conversations could be pureed in peace, sautéed in self-control, and julienned in joy. That sounds far more digestible for the recipients of our offerings, as well as for our own digestive tracts.

I tend to have an acidic interior, so I have to watch my intake of tomatoes, coffee, and vinegar. I also can react to others with an acidic nip to my words, if my fruit-filters aren't in place. But when I have had a worthwhile, uplifting conversation with someone, I leave with a satisfied feeling.

Recently while sitting in a coffee shop, I became aware of customers' wafting conversations at two nearby tables. Okay, okay, I was deliberately listening in, but we were in such close proximity I could hardly help myself.

At one table sat an older man obviously mentoring a younger man. The younger of the two had papers spread on the tiny table as well as in his lap, and as the older man theorized, the other took copious notes. The topic seemed to stem from the problems that minorities face in our school systems and the current efforts to correct that.

Two college-aged men were at the other table. They were almost nose to nose in an intense conversation. Despite the similarity in their ages, one was coaching the other in his school priorities and in managing his time and studies.

I love that we live in a time where mentoring, coaching, cheerleading, and guiding others seem to thrive. What a fruit-filled opportunity that allows us to both learn and to invest wisely in others.

It's a calling for all ages. Scripture mentions that the older are to train the younger, and we are all older than someone. Come to think of it, these days I'm older than most . . . that kind of snuck up on me.

Here's the great news about our boomerang words. When they drip with honey, they allow us to receive a double health benefit of sweetness. It's like double coupon day. We can't go wrong.

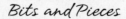

Bits and Pieces

1. When was the last time you felt your words rumble around inside of you? What was the occasion?
2. What kind of words add life to your well-being?
3. What kind of word filter do you use? Has it been effective?
4. When are you acidic in what you say?
5. Whom do you mentor? Why? If you're not mentoring someone, why not?
6. Who is your mentor? Why?
7. When was your last sweet conversation?

Held to the Light

The words of his mouth were smoother than butter, but war was in his heart; his words were softer than oil, yet they were drawn swords. (Psalm 55:21)

How sweet are Your words to my taste, sweeter than honey to my mouth! (Psalm 119:103)

Let the words of my mouth and the meditation of my heart be acceptable in Your sight, O LORD, my strength and my Redeemer. (Psalm 19:14)

Your words were found, and I ate them, and Your word was to me the joy and rejoicing of my heart; for I am called by Your name, O LORD God of hosts. (Jeremiah 15:16)

CHAPTER 10

Expiration Dates

Listen to counsel and receive instruction, that you
may be wise in your latter days.

—PROVERBS 19:20

I couldn't believe my eyes. Clearly marked on the end of the egg carton was the expiration date "Mar 19," and this was May 6. How could that be? I knew my hubby had picked up the carton while I was out of town over the weekend . . . so where did he get it? Goodwill? Antique Alley?

My first thought was that some store was pawning off their old stock, and Les hadn't paid close enough attention. (Aren't I just a font of trust?) Turned out I was wrong on both accounts. Yes, wrong again. Les had stopped at a friend's house, and since the couple raises chickens, they had shared their egg basket with him. They put the new harvest in an old carton for him to carry home and, thus, the expiration date.

One of the things I love about God's Word is that it has no expiration date. It's as fresh today as it was when Solomon penned the proverbs. And it will remain fresh (crisp, invigorating, vibrant) throughout time and eternity. It has no potential to wilt, sour, or spoil.

Therefore, to *listen* and *receive* that kind of unblemished counsel just makes sense.

That would be unlike the facial wrinkle-removing apparatus my friend Gladys (not her real name) bought after listening to the fast talk of a television hype woman.

When Gladys's order appeared on her doorstep, she quickly hid it in her closet so no one would know. She had a big shindig to attend, and Gladys wanted to look her spiffiest. In preparation, she took to her walk-in closet daily, lest someone catch her, as she began her secret treatments.

She had fallen prey to the advertising late one night when sleep was about to overtake her. Gladys's eyelids must have draped down over a good portion of her brain because when she heard the come-hither voice on television—touting the miracle effects of this toylike, hand-held device—she reached for the phone and ordered it. A short time after it arrived, Gladys realized it was just another fountain-of-youth plastic ploy, meant to deceive and bilk the vain and the aging. (I confess, I fall into both categories.) My friend would be the first to laugh at herself. We have confessed to each other how gullible we both can be at times.

Gullibility that ends in giggles is one thing, but when you lose your innocence to a trusted date, your life savings to a swindler, or your heart to a rascal, all the humor is drained out of gullibility.

We all need sound counsel that will protect us from our own tendencies and other people's corrupt intentions. God's Word makes even the foolish appear wise when they listen and receive. I should know. I was a foolish young woman, full of my own opinions that I held onto as if they were gossamer wings that could help me to fly. When, instead of gaining altitude, I crashed, my pride was broken enough that my opinions began to seep out. Gradually, I replaced them with God's counsel as I listened to His Word and received it into my needy life.

Becoming a listener is a huge change for many of us who are so interested in what we are about to say that we even talk over others to get our two cents in. (Although I've noticed of late that I tend to do it because I'm afraid I'll forget what I was going to say.)

If you're given to outbreaks of chattiness, here is my suggestion: Become a stenographer. Carry a notebook and write down what you hear God saying to your heart.

Some of you may be wondering, what if you don't hear anything? Record that too. God made the silence. It has its own mysterious ministry to our lives. It's often in the quiet spaces we hear our own thoughts, which can be deeply revealing. Chatter can be a cover for haunting fear, seething anger, troubling insecurity, or embedded pain. Of course, it also can be a sign of pride and self-importance, a belief that what we have to say is more important than others, or an indication of our own shallowness, proving that the pond isn't very deep.

I find that often God speaks to me through His Word. Not always. But often. And there are times after reading when I think that I didn't receive anything, but then later what didn't seem to matter to me in the moment comes back to my ear as fresh counsel. In the midst of a discussion or in answer to a puzzling question, I hear myself saying, "Well, in Deuteronomy it says . . ."

I love the close of this proverb when it promises that truth stays with us into our latter years. Latter. Doesn't that sound, uh, ancient, as in almost finished, kaput? Careful, don't misread it. It's not *ladder*, as in what you lean against the house to clean out the gutters. No, by the time we get to "latter," our ladder doesn't usually reach the second floor; we are a few rungs short, and our gutters are clogged . . . if you know what I mean. Which is why we especially need the stabilizing strength wisdom brings us.

When we climb the ladder of counsel and instruction, we are guaranteed the latter wisdom . . . with no expiration date!

Bits and Pieces

1. Why is listening easier than receiving?
2. Have you ever ordered something that was a waste of money? What was it? How did that make you feel?
3. What three personal "tendencies" do you need to be protected from?
4. What are three ways silence is a ministry to your heart?
5. Are you a good listener? Why or why not?
6. When are our latter years?
7. Why do expiration dates matter?
8. In what ways might you consider yourself wise? In what ways unwise?

Held to the Light

But if they had stood in My counsel, and had caused My people to hear My words, then they would have turned them from their evil way and from the evil of their doings. (Jeremiah 23:22)

Listen now to my voice; I will give you counsel, and God will be with you: Stand before God for the people, so that you may bring difficulties to God. (Exodus 18:19)

Have you heard the counsel of God? Do you limit wisdom to yourself? (Job 15:8)

All scripture is given by inspiration of God, and is profitable for doctrine, for reproof, for correction, for instruction in righteousness, that the man [woman] of God may be complete, throroughly equipped for every good work. (2 Timothy 3:16–17)

Take counsel together, but it will come to nothing; speak the word, but it will not stand, for God is with us. (Isaiah 8:10)

CHAPTER 11

Tower of Strength

The name of the Lord is a strong tower.

—PROVERBS 18:10*a*

I love that our triune God has within His name fathomless definition. He is incomprehensibly endless. He is incalculable.

Because of God's immeasurability, we, while Earth-bound, can never finish searching out who the Lord is and how He works out evil for good and death for eternal life. Although we can't figure out or reason through many of God's mysteries, He does allow us to experience Him as much as we are willing. He invites us into a divine fullness, which will come to completion just the other side of life's veil.

I've learned that knowing even one of the Lord's names doesn't guarantee I actually "get it" until I have occasion to witness or partake of it. For instance, He is our Comforter, which I believed by faith, but it wasn't until I went through great personal tragedy that I experienced it firsthand. The Lord comforts us supernaturally by His Spirit—that palpable inner awareness of safety and purpose that we sense but can't explain. He also uses His people in a myriad of ways to intersect our lives at just the right moments. Then there's God's creation, which can soothe our angst and teach us truths.

Even though the Lord isn't hampered by time, He often uses time frames in our lives to bring about healing resolve. His endlessly comforting ministry continues toward us through printed words, prayer, music, dreams, and ordained events, to name a few of the diverse ways He loves on us.

I came to know His name as Shepherd during my agoraphobic years when, as a lost lamb, I was cornered by the wolf of fear. As I cried out to be rescued, I became aware of gentle yet deliberate nudges from His shepherd's staff, encouraging me to head for the gate. His tender care for my shivering emotions helped to steady me while I wobbled toward freedom.

The Lord continues to teach me His name as the Light of the World by shining understanding into my muddled mind when I'm unclear about what to do next. He illuminates my path with His Word, holy promptings, and harmonic counselors.

Last year, when my best friend, Carol, died, I initially experienced a heightened awareness of the Lord's shining presence in our heartbroken midst. But as the days unfolded into months, I found myself in the dark tunnel of grief, fumbling about in search of a lantern. To be honest, I didn't want a bright verse, a shiny song, or a brand-spanking-new friend. What I wanted was Carol back in my daily life where she belonged and had been for more than fifty years. My resistance to God's ordained plan kept me stumbling into deep caverns of sadness.

I believe with all my heart that grief is a necessary, shadowed labyrinth we must walk through, and I also believe we can delay it with our resistance. I didn't want to light the lantern of relinquishment, which would have implied that what God had done in taking Carol was okay. It would never feel right, yet it was necessary for me to reach that place of bending my knee to God's sovereignty if I was to find my way back into the light He offered.

If we don't eventually step out of our anguish, it can lead to mental illness, spiritual apathy, physical disease, and a tainted view of God. Grieving, while a process we must go through, never was intended to be our address. Yes, we may walk with a limp the rest of our days, but the seething part of agony can be transformed into wise compassion.

You can see with my current struggles why, of all the Lord's names, I have chosen to ponder Comforter, Shepherd, and the Light of the World. And you can also see why I was drawn to this verse about God being our strong tower. This life gives us reason to seek refuge, and I'm grateful to say that God offers us that in the tower of His names.

Bits and Pieces

1. What are your favorite names of God?
2. Define *fathomless*. Use it in a sentence three different ways.
3 What do you find mysterious about God?
4. Which of God's names from Scripture do you "get"? How did you get it?
5. When have you encountered the wolf of fear?
6. Have you experienced a holy prompting? What is the difference between that and a good idea?
7. Why can't we predict when others should be through their grieving?
8. Why do you think a strong tower is one of the pictures of who God is?
9. Which name of God are you learning about now in your life?

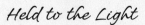

Held to the Light

The God of my strength, in whom I will trust; my shield and the horn of my salvation, my stronghold and my refuge; my Savior, You save me from violence. (2 Samuel 22:3)

For you have been a shelter for me, a strong tower from the enemy. (Psalm 61:3)

In God is my salvation and my glory; the rock of my strength, and my refuge, is in God. (Psalm 62:7)

God is our refuge and strength, a very present help in trouble. (Psalm 46:1)

My lovingkindness and my fortress, my high tower and my deliverer, my shield and the One in whom I take refuge. (Psalm 144:2)

CHAPTER 12

Get Smart

Whoever loves instruction loves knowledge, but he who hates correction is stupid.

—PROVERBS 12:1

Emily, a friend of mine, had worked for a company for a number of years as a project manager supervisor, when the company downsized dramatically. Emily's position was eliminated, but she was retained and given new areas of responsibility and different titles, including office manager and staff accountant. At first she felt demoted, but as she reassessed her circumstances, she realized she was fortunate still to be employed. Since these positions were unfamiliar territory for her, Emily quickly learned to listen and to receive instruction. Wanting to remain employed, she was highly motivated to accept knowledge and correction from others, which was more desirable than standing in unemployment lines.

Ever notice how sometimes we have to be forced to be smart? Sometimes we need a motivating nudge.

For instance, I have plantar fasciitis, which is a painful foot ailment. Did I say painful? Try excruciating. If I understand correctly, the affliction is caused by a tear and inflammation of the muscle that runs from the bottom of one's toes, across the bottom of the foot, and then up the back of the leg. The main pain is in the arch and heel. It feels as though someone is hammering a nail—correction, make that a spike—into the heel.

It has taken this level of discomfort to force me to decide that high heels might not be the best footwear for me. Brilliant, huh? I'm a fast learner, yessiree.

It turned out that several of my friends have had this ailment and went to great lengths to find relief and recovery. Trust me when I say I leaned in to hear their hard-earned instructions and then hobbled home to give their knowledge a try in hopes of shortening my own recovery (and not being stupid by ignoring their advice).

One of my friends found the most relief with a night-time stretch sock; in fact, she had one sent to me overnight. It stretches tightly all the way to the knee, and then a long strip of Velcro pulls up the front of the leg through a ring and then folds back over itself, causing the toes to be pulled heaven-ward. Think Will Ferrell in *Elf.* Uh-huh. Did I mind? Nope. I just wanted resolution, and if that meant I had to look like an elderly dork in search of Santa Claus when I climbed into bed, that worked for me. My husband . . . not so much.

My second friend told me about a plastic rocking imple-ment that helped her. Think rocking horse for the foot. I ordered it, and when it arrived, I attempted to use it, but I could hardly get up on it, much less rock it. Athleticism isn't my strongest suit. Turned out my $5^{1}/_{2}$-sized foot was too small for the design, and it added pressure in the wrong areas.

Then I tried working out on a stationary bike. Not only didn't that help, but also one night, after a forty-five-minute pedaling session, my legs jammed up with charley horses. I had never had that many at once, and over the last five years, honey, I've had plenty. I find Charley highly motivational. He makes me dance (a frantic boogie-woogie) and howl at the same time, while also deepening my prayer life. It's in the height of those cramping moments that I volunteer to pick ticks off gorillas in the jungle for Jesus if the pain will just stop.

Honestly, I could never figure out why that kind of agony is called a charley horse. First off, who wants to be on a first-name basis with a guy who causes that kind of torture? And second, I could no more sling my leg over a saddle or go for a trot, when my leg is knotted in piercing pain, than I could outrun a gazelle.

The following morning, a third friend, on hearing my charley-horse saga, said she had a cure for my leg cramps. Okay, this is where you need to hold on to your pantaloons because this is a humdinger of a remedy. Ready? Soap. Yup, a bar of soap. You put it between the sheets, down by your feet and legs, and then go to sleep. No, I'm not kidding, and yes, I know it sounds crazy, but, hey, I couldn't go wrong because, if it didn't work, I could take a bath to make the soap worth my while. Actually, though, I haven't had a leg cramp since the week I tried it. Coincidence? Perhaps. But I'm keeping my soap in the nightstand just in case.

Warning: Don't leave soap between sheets on wash day. If you inadvertently toss the wad of sheets in the washer with the soap bar, all I can say is, expect results.

Speaking of results, if we want to improve our IQs, we need to pursue, embrace, and not let go of instruction, realizing it leads to knowledge. Let's be big enough to not see correction as something that causes us to feel small, but let's allow it to make us smart.

Bits and Pieces

1. Have you ever lost a job? How did that make you feel?
2. When was the last time you were corrected?
3. What feelings or memories did that evoke?
4. What did you learn?

5. Do you "love" being instructed?
6. What odd remedy have you tried?
7. When were you in the worst physical pain?
8. When do you think our learning curve stops?

Held to the Light

He also opens their ear to instruction, and commands that they turn from iniquity. (Job 36:10)

Receive, please, instruction from His mouth, and lay up His words in your heart. (Job 22:22)

And let our people also learn to maintain good works, to meet urgent needs, that they may not be unfruitful. (Titus 3:14)

And a servant of the Lord must not quarrel but be gentle to all, able to teach, patient. (2 Timothy 2:24)

Teach me Your way, O Lord; I will walk in your truth; unite my heart to fear Your name. (Psalm 86:11)

CHAPTER 13

An Encounter with Ruby

For wisdom is more precious than rubies, and all the things one may desire cannot be compared with her.

—PROVERBS 8:11

Ruby is a sensation! Everybody says so. She is vibrant, warm, vivid, and promotes love wherever she goes. She is multifaceted in her international appeal and is accustomed to royalty. I personally am drawn to her sanguine charm. Quite honestly, Ruby's a gem! Really. No, really, I'm speaking of the gem.

Did you know this fiery gemstone generally is mined in Burma—although the darker and violet-red rubies come principally from Thailand? Rubies are the hardest mineral second to the diamond and require expert care to cut.

For a long time rubies were primarily from India and were so treasured that rulers, on hearing a particularly beautiful ruby had been found, would send out dignitaries to meet and escort the gemstone. Wouldn't you love to be treated that way? C'mon, really.

One of the world's largest and finest rubies is displayed at the Smithsonian National Museum of Natural History and weights in at 23.1 carats.

I own a ruby cross. People who are drawn to it will move in close, squint their eyes, and ask, "Are those rubies?" Collectively my rubies weigh in at, oh, probably a butterfly's whisper.

The Smithsonian's gemstone is a Burmese ruby, set in a diamond-arrayed platinum ring. A philanthropist in memory of his wife, Carmen Lúcia, donated it to the museum. Aw, what a romantic way to honor her name.

I wonder what my hubby would donate in my name. *Hmm,* never mind . . . a bobblehead just flitted through my thoughts, or a pair of those wind-up teeth that chatter endlessly. Some mines are better left unexplored.

One thing we know for sure: rubies are a valued treasure.

Scripture tells us that we would be wealthier if, instead of gathering rubies, we became aficionados of wisdom by passionately chipping away in the rich-veined mines of God's Word to accrue true wealth. This wealth is stored up within for us to use to live passionately and to invest generously in others.

Wisdom has its own vibrancy. I've seen that in the lives of those who display it . . . not from a lit case but from a lit life. I love to encounter wise people, those who have done their homework and are living in ways that illuminate what they believe.

Rich Stearns, the president of World Vision, is such a person. He has written a book called *The Hole in Our Gospel*, in which he shares his reluctant response to give up a flourishing corporate position for a risky step into the lives of the poor throughout the world. Rich confesses his hesitancy to leave behind his comfortable lifestyle and how two questions motivated him forward: "What does God expect of me? Am I willing to do God's will?"

The answer to those questions has changed Rich's life and his perspective on what matters. Because of his willingness to respond to God's voice and to live out his calling with gusto, we onlookers are taken aback by the sheer beauty of sacrifices well timed and energies well spent.

Here's a stunning aspect of Rich's change of heart—the focus of his efforts isn't on him but on the needs of the poor. There's something about ministries that are focused on the struggles in our world and not on the leadership personalities that's appealing and comforting in our slick, star-studded society.

Wisdom is winsome. It's love-based. It resonates with morality, resounds with truth, restores dignity, and reforms the heart. And it gives us something to say that's worth hearing.

Speaking of worth hearing, listen to this line from the life of Samuel Rutherford, one of the most influential Scottish Presbyterians in the Westminster Assembly, who was persecuted for his beliefs: "Jesus Christ came into my prison cell last night and every stone flashed like a ruby."

No matter our circumstances—whether we are on a throne, in a third-world country among the poor, on a board of directors, or in a prison cell—treasured wisdom will counsel our heads and comfort our hearts.

Now, that's brilliant!

Bits and Pieces

1. What rubies do you own? How do they compare to the Smithsonian's?
2. Have you ever made a donation in memory of someone? If so, who?
3. Have you ever chipped away and found a ruby in God's Word? If so, where is it located?
4. Who do you know who lives a "lit life?"
5. What does God expect of you?
6. Are you willing to do God's will?
7. What event in your life caused you to witness stones like rubies?

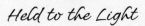

Held to the Light

Get wisdom! (Proverbs 4:5a)

Christ, in whom are written all the treasures of wisdom. (Colossians 2:2–3)

And Jesus increased in wisdom and stature, and in favor with God and men. (Luke 2:52)

The ear that hears the rebukes of life will abide among the wise. (Proverbs 15:31)

Who can find a virtuous wife? For her worth is far above rubies. (Proverbs 31:10)

CHAPTER 14

Dem Bones, Dem Bones

A good report makes the bones healthy.

—PROVERBS 15:30*b*

Help! I need some good reports pronto! The old bones are getting creaky.

When I hear good news, it makes me stand taller, prouder, and feel more resilient . . . as though I want to skip. Even though my bones aren't that flexible any longer, my heart still spryly skips within me when I hear a noteworthy report.

Speaking of news, did you know that at birth we have around 350 bones, but by the time we've hopscotched our way to adulthood, we're down to 206 bones? Okay, so how did those 144 bones just up and disappear? Well, actually they don't rattle off to haunt a graveyard; they fuse within us, bringing down the individual count. That's why babies are more flexible than adults—they aren't all connected yet.

I know some adults who don't seem connected. I mean, have you ever thought someone was a real bonehead? C'mon now, be honest. I know I have. Like the guy on the airplane who clunked me in the head with his two loaves of French bread and then snarled at me for what he had done. Now, he was a bit of a bonehead. A big bit. Or the young teen on a school bus who gave me an obscene gesture as I drove behind the vehicle. To his surprise I was waiting for him when he de-boarded so that we might have a chat.

But to tell the truth, we all are boneheads in the sense that the skull contains twenty-eight bones. Eight are cranial, fourteen are facial, and six are ear bones.

Who knew the diminutive ear was so bony? I do know that the tiniest bone in the body—called the *stirrup*—is housed in the ear; when I was young, my mom had surgery on it to correct a hearing problem. It was a grand success, proving once again that little things really do matter. The stirrup is only three millimeters; yet when that bone isn't healthy, the world becomes a muffled, if not silent, place.

Guess where we have the most bones? No, try again.

It's our hands: twenty-six bones in each one for a whopping total of fifty-two.

My oldest son almost lessened that number when he slipped last year while using an electric saber saw. Ouch! Fortunately, surgery put Humpty Dumpty back together again.

This weekend my youngest son had an unfortunate encounter with a forklift and his pinkie finger. It's still attached but is bulbous and badly bruised. One really forgets how valuable all these bones are until they are threatened or fractured, and then we're reminded of their amazing benefits.

I was on an international flight to Africa when I lunged forward against my seat belt in an attempt to reach a magazine on takeoff. I heard a pop and simultaneously felt a slicing pain rip across my rib cage. I sat perfectly still, realizing there was a good chance I had snapped a rib.

During the trip and for weeks afterward, if I breathed too deeply, sneezed, or tried to reach up or down, my rib cage filed an immediate grievance against me. While in Africa, I carried a pillow to support my ribs as we bounced around in Land Rovers, traipsed down windy paths, and flew in a hot air balloon. It took time, but eventually I recovered with a new appreciation for my bone-riddled rib cage.

I'm told working out helps our bones strengthen, as do the right foods and supplements. But still my favorite health aid for our frame is the prescription given to us by the One who formed us (Eve from a rib, mind you). Really, who would know better? God tells us that good news makes our skeletal frames healthier. From our bony heads, to our back bones, to our hands, to our femurs (longest bone), right down to our smallest toe, we absorb good news as it shoots through our bones like high doses of vitamins C, E, and calcium.

Good news isn't exactly prevalent on TV or in the papers. We have to count on each other for that.

In fact, my assistant, Amy, recently the bearer of good news, returned from a trip with this story. While flying to her destination, she met Cindy, who shared that she was a bone marrow donor. Cindy saw a blood drive at a community center one day and decided to donate blood. They asked her if she would be willing to donate her bone marrow if she was ever a match, and Cindy said yes. This woman's grandmother had died recently, and Cindy's loss was fresh on her mind. She thought if she ever had the chance to help someone else live, she would.

Three years went by before Cindy's phone rang. The person on the other end told her that she was a match for someone and asked if she was still willing to be a donor. Without hesitation Cindy agreed. She went through the harvesting of her marrow but was given no information about the recipient.

A year later, Cindy received the news that because of her willingness, the recipient had survived and now wanted to meet Cindy. Her airfare paid by the recipient, Cindy flew out east to meet this woman and her family members, who were lined up to personally thank the donor. It turned out that because of Cindy's generosity, the patient lived to see her first grandchild born. Family members told Cindy that she would never know what it meant to each of them when they received the good news that a donor match had been found.

Are you a donor of good news? I have to work at it. I'm sort of an optimistic pessimist if you know what I mean. Without the girding up of my mind, I can become a gloomy forecaster. Girding my mind requires deliberately cinching my thoughts into place so they align with God's higher thoughts. I find I need to keep my six ear bones attuned to His Word if I'm to be the bearer of a good report. When that happens, why, even bad news sounds better.

Bits and Pieces

1. What was the last news you heard that made you want to skip?
2. Have you ever broken a bone? How long did it take to heal?
3. Why do little things matter?
4. When have you been a bonehead?
5. What good news have you spread recently? To whom did you share it?

Held to the Light

And Adam said: "This is now bone of my bones and flesh of my flesh." (Genesis 2:23a)

Again He said to me, "Prophesy to these bones, and say to them, 'O dry bones, hear the word of the LORD!'" (Ezekiel 37:4)

When I kept silent, my bones grew old through my groaning all the day long. (Psalm 32:3)

For these things were done that the Scripture should be fulfilled, "Not one of His bones shall be broken." (John 19:36)

Pleasant words are like a honeycomb, sweetness to the soul and health to the bones. (Proverbs 16:24)

CHAPTER 15

Simple Acts of Kindness

He who has a generous eye will be blessed, for he gives of his bread to the poor.

—PROVERBS 22:9

Acts of generosity move me, especially those done with nothing in mind but to help another living soul. No applause sought, no credit needed.

A teenage friend of mine felt God told her during prayer time to go to a nearby park and feed the hungry. She informed her mom, who immediately collected up food to support her daughter's obedience. Then friends who heard the plan joined in, and soon a posse of young people, under the supervision of a mom, converged on the park with bags of food that they handed out to grateful people.

I love that simple act of love. Were there people at the park who didn't deserve a handout? Maybe. All I know is I was an undeserving soul, but Christ, the Bread of Life, fed me.

My friend Randy has a sensitive heart, an observant eye, and a willing spirit when it comes to reaching out to assist others, especially the unfortunate and the disadvantaged. He is part of a small band of friends who travel together to conferences, and I'm fortunate to be one of those. The reason I say "fortunate" is because I know if I have a need, Randy will be there to help. As a group, we know that when Randy suddenly disappears, he probably has spotted someone, a stranger, who has dropped something, is struggling to lift something, or needs assistance getting to his or her seat on the plane. We have watched him rescue children in their clumsiness, the handicapped with their limitations, and the elderly in their confusion (yes, that would be me).

It must please God to bless Randy.

My son Marty impresses me by the way he generously uses his practical skills to help others. He is the one folks call in the middle of the winter when their heat goes out and in the scorching summer when the air-conditioning goes kaput. He's the guy on someone else's roof because it has sprung a leak causing the ceiling tile to land in the spaghetti. Marty's the one who crawls through musty attics in search of unwanted critters even though he hates tight places. He's the guy who will run for the pizza, change your tire, and after a long day of work, take his restless, car-loving dog for a ride.

Oh, and did I mention, before Marty leaves our home, he always kisses his mom. Aw.

If a contest existed for the King of Random Acts of Kindness, my husband, Les, would have to be chosen. He is one of the most generous people I know. Sure, I'm partial, but literally hundreds of people have verified this as well. In fact, recently Les took an Amtrak trip to see his doctors in Chicago. Later a woman wrote me a note referring to him as the Angel of Amtrak. Why, even Les's doctors love his playful heart and his corny jokes, which he lavishes on others everywhere he goes. His generous humor matches his acts of helpfulness because he loves to leave people laughing, and I've had forty-seven years of marriage to this funny man to verify that he does. Les can't pass up a lemonade stand hosted by future entrepreneurs; his generous contribution leaves them awestruck and motivated.

God has given us a gazillion ways to be generous with our time, talent, and our tamale soup. Yup, what's better than an unexpected steaming dinner dropped off on our doorstep? Especially if someone has been laid off, is going through a current loss, is ill, or is new to a neighborhood.

The poor may include those who are struggling for direction, can't pay their utility bill, or need clothes for the kids. I remember years ago when our family hit hard times, and a man from our church bought our son a coat for the new school year. May I just say, in Michigan coats are necessary. I've never forgotten that act of generosity.

Be creative and extravagant! Find ways to spend your gifts, your monies, and your time to bless others. The soul of the tight-fisted withers while the one who lavishes on others waters generational roots.

Whether you write a note of encouragement, drop a few dollars in an envelope, utter a heartfelt prayer, offer a helping hand, lend a listening ear, or plant a big ol' kiss, be alert to the poor and give, give, give.

Bits and Pieces

1. List three small acts of generosity extended to you that have meant the world.
2. When was the last time you assisted a stranger? How did you do that?
3. What would you do if you had the chance to bless a person you thought didn't deserve it?
4. What skills, gifts, or abilities do you have that could be used to help others?
5. Define *poor*.
6. Make a list of people who you believe are poor. How might you help them?

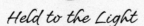

Held to the Light

Therefore, as the elect of God, holy and beloved, put on tender mercies, kindness, humility, meekness, longsuffering. (Colossians 3:12)

Every man shall give as he is able, according to the blessing of the LORD your God which He has given you. (Deuteronomy 16:17)

Freely you have received, freely give. (Matthew 10:8b)

A present is a precious stone in the eyes of its possessor. (Proverbs 17:8a)

CHAPTER 16

Fading Flowers

Beauty is passing.

—PROVERBS 31:30*b*

Beauty is passing...that's for sure. Like NASCAR at Indy, I might add. Honestly, the etched person in my mirror was only yesterday a freckle-faced, pigtailed, munchkin on a tricycle. But now she's Granny from Clampett fame (*The Beverly Hillbillies*) in a rocker, strapped on the back of a pickup.

I'm not just talking about how fast time goes by, but how quickly appearances change. When I was a kid, I'd ask my dad for something, and if he felt it was unreasonable, he would quip, "Have you got a screw loose?" So now I'm wondering if that's why my knees have gathered at my ankles; my bottom has slid into my thighs; my chin has suffered a landslide, ruffling my neck; and my underarms are so, uh, flexible, I almost knocked myself out the other day waving to a neighbor. Maybe if I go to the place where screws are adjusted, I could have things tightened so they would hike back up into their rightful places.

But people-beauty is not the only fading flower. Take the *Paeonia lactiflora*, also known as the peony. Its stunning double blooms and heady fragrance make it a showstopper. But in the time it takes to curtsy, its blooms have come and gone. Peonies inspire poems and paintings and transform novice shutterbugs into professional photographers.

I had multiple peony bushes at my last home, and in the spring when they bloomed, I could be seen sprinting around the house in search of my camera. Then I would go out to take shots from every possible angle. Finally I would collect up an armful of ant-covered cuttings and head for the kitchen, where these romantic blossoms would be arranged and adored. (Yes, I shook off the critters into the grass first.) Outside, though, one burst of wind or a quick thunderstorm, and the bushes would quickly give up their beauty, as the petals collected at the base of the bushes, looking like discarded petticoats.

Beauty . . . it passes.

A sight that was beautiful to my husband's eyes was a small, white, wooden church in his hometown in the Upper Peninsula of Michigan; it flooded him with childhood memories. Hours of "why, when I was growing up" stories would follow on every vacation as soon as Les spotted its steeple . . . yes, hours. Then one year we returned to his hometown, and the church was gone. Les was heartsick.

"If only I had known, I would have bought the bell or purchased a piece of property and had the church moved to save it," he has said many times since.

Ah, but beauty doesn't last . . . at least not here, not yet.

A sunrise fills the world with hope, but before we can finish a song about its beauty, the sun has risen high into the sky and has become a blinding force we take shelter from. Then, as the crimson sun sets, we sit holding our breath, knowing that if we dare to breathe, it will dissolve into the ocean's edge and spill over the horizon.

As the horizon darkens, the fireflies scurry out into the early evening with their diminutive lanterns, helping to keep the landscape lit. These little dashes of light have been flitting about in the summer heat forever. Well, at least *my* forever. I'm being told now that they are dying off. Huh? How can that be? Is it because beauty doesn't last?

I find this theme troubling. Because God has set eternity in our hearts, we want what is good, lovely, and beautiful to last. And we are promised it will, one day.

One glorious day, God will establish a new heaven and a new earth, and it will have no need of the sun or moon, for the "glory of God" will illuminate it (Revelation 21:23*b*). The Lamb will be the light.

And guess what? That beauty is indelible.

Bits and Pieces

1. What can you add to my list of the way our appearance changes over the years?
2. What purpose do you think nature plays in our lives?
3. Why do you think we are drawn to the art of nature?
4. What beauty have you seen fade?
5. How does that make you feel?
6. What have you found in this life to be indelible?

Held to the Light

Then adorn yourself with majesty and splendor, and array yourself with glory and beauty. (Job 40:10)

And the glorious beauty is a fading flower which is at the head of the verdant valley. (Isaiah 28:4a)

And let the beauty of the LORD our God be upon us. (Psalm 90:17a)

Worship the LORD in the beauty of holiness. (Psalm 29:2b)

CHAPTER 17

Tools of the Trade

The wise woman builds her house.

—PROVERBS 14:1*a*

The men in my world—hubby, two adult sons, two young grandsons—are all about tools. I always know what I can buy them at holiday time. Whether it's a gadget for the garage, kitchen, or barbecue, it's a surefire way to make points. One Christmas, Les gave our sons each a fancy-dancy, fully loaded toolbox, and I must say I never saw either of them levitate over a gift like they did over that metal chest of boy-toys.

Les, who is into stained glass, requires a trip to a specialty shop to purchase his tools of choice: offset pliers, glass grinders, and glass cutters. My eldest son, Marty, is an electrician and also has very specific tool needs: ohmmeters, wire strippers, and outlet testers. My nine-year-old grandson, Justin, is the easiest to buy for since his tools of preference include boxes of crayons, notepads, pencils, and bags of M&M's . . . to maintain his strength. I so get that.

When I thought about different kinds of tools, I remembered this proverb about a woman building her house. It reminded me that women, too, have need of a select kit for the building up of their homes. So I rustled around in my toolbox and found a few tools that have helped me to be wise through my forty-seven years of marriage and forty-four years of motherhood.

Faith: My faith in Christ is the cornerstone of my life and my home. I confess I haven't always been the sweetest wife or the most hormonally consistent mom, but because Christ was the bottom line in our family's relationships, we have all survived each other.

Life isn't easy, relationships are testy, and circumstances aren't predictable, but Christ is bedrock. When Les and I have been stuck in the muck of a disagreement, it has been Christ's intervention that has caused our stalemate to move to a place of negotiation. When the kids and I have been at odds, it has been Christ's presence that has restored harmony. When we as a family were broke and needy, it was Christ's generosity that restored our hope.

Love: Because love covers "a multitude of sins" (1 Peter 4:8*b*), it's the perfect all-purpose tool for our kits. When all else fails, pull out love, and you will find it is able to do what no other tool can accomplish: it adjusts attitudes, hammers defenses, calibrates perspectives, and covers offenses. Better yet, pull out love first, and we can watch how the whole climate of our home is transformed before things escalate. Love makes us prettier, calmer, smarter, more reasonable, more sensitive, and certainly more approachable.

Once in a while my travel schedule will be so congested that I find it hard to fit in fun time with my grandsons. During one of those go-go spells, I grabbed a visit with Justin. He gave me multiple hugs and said, "Nana, I don't get to see you anymore. What's up with that?"

His loving concern made me giggle. What's up with that, indeed?

Humor: This is an essential tool that securely fastens down good mental health and helps to establish social savvy. Laughter disarms, relaxes, distracts, enhances, and connects us to one another. There is no sweeter melody than when our families laugh together, and sharing joy causes us to bond at the heart. Laughter assuages hostilities that can flare quickly amid daily family dynamics. So I recommend keeping this tool close at hand and using it liberally.

Forgiveness: I keep saying each tool is essential, and quite honestly, the ones I've mentioned are, and this one is no exception. People hurt people. That's just the way it goes in this kick-the-can world. And the more we care for someone, the deeper the potential for injuring that person. We set an unfair expectation on others when we're shocked that they hurt and disappoint us. We add insult to injury when we then shame them for their behavior. Of course, no one wants to be hurt, but hurt is as much a part of our human condition as hiccups or bad breath. Sooner or later, everyone disappoints everyone. God said we would do that to each other. That makes forgiveness key to a family's ongoing survival. We live in each other's cul-de-sacs, so we're bound to run into one another with our rusty Studebaker stubbornness and our noisy Model-T tempers.

Sometimes we may need a complete overhaul to forgive someone when we have been deeply offended. Only one Mechanic has the know-how and tools to drain the oil of resentment from our hearts, adjust our cracked-heart carburetors, realign our spinning wheels, and fill us up with the fuel it will take to make it all the way home.

A note to any of you in an abusive family relationship: Forgiveness isn't an excuse to allow degrading treatment to continue. God values you. God cherishes you. He doesn't want you battered. Go to a safe place, get help, and learn how to live with boundaries in place and your dignity intact. And yes, you will need to forgive, but from a safe distance; don't put yourself back in harm's way, thinking God wants you to be hurt. Find someone who can help you to think wisely.

Faith, love, humor, and forgiveness are God-given tools that help us to build our homes and to make us wise . . . very wise.

Bits and Pieces

1. Who are the men in your life?
2. What's in your tool kit?
3. In what ways have you been a sweet wife? In what ways might you have been a not-so-sweet wife?
4. How have you been a hormonally consistent mom? How do you express your hormonal imbalance with your family?
5. How did you work through finding forgiveness for yourself when you were less than sweet or hormonally inconsistent?
6. Do you think any of these four tools (faith, love, humor, forgiveness) are more important than the others? Why?
7. What do you do to maintain your strength?
8. How can you facilitate your family's laughing together?
9. What family member do you need to forgive?
10. In what ways would you describe yourself as a wise woman?

Held to the Light

As the Father loved me, I also have loved you; abide in My love. (John 15:9)

The LORD your God in your midst, the Mighty One, will save; He will rejoice over you with gladness, He will quiet you with His love, He will rejoice over you with singing. (Zephaniah 3:17)

Then our mouth was filled with laughter, and our tongue with singing. (Psalm 126:2a)

"Lord, how often shall my brother sin against me, and I forgive him? Up to seven times?" Jesus said to him, "I do not say to you, up to seven times, but up to seventy times seven." (Matthew 18:21–22)

I have fought the good fight, I have finished the race, I have kept the faith. (2 Timothy 4:7)

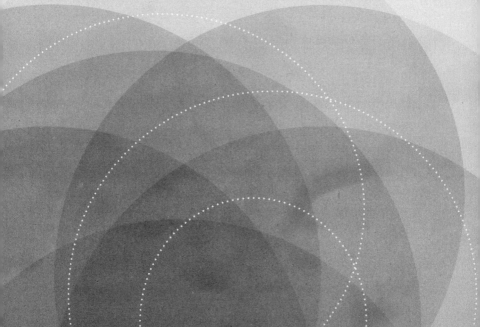

CHAPTER 18

A Picture vs. a Thousand Words

Apply your heart to instruction.

—PROVERBS 23:12*a*

I'm not good with printed instructions . . . unless they're illustrated. Yup, I'm one of those big kids who need pictures. I have a collection of cookbooks, but my favorite ones have an abundance of illustrations. Now, I'm not suggesting that they are used a lot—there are no sweet potato skid marks left on the pages from my last soufflé—but if I were to feel so inclined, I'd be far more likely to whip up a hollandaise sauce or a meringue if the recipes were accompanied by a pictorial guide.

When I was young, my parents bought me a set of encyclopedias, and even though scattered pictures appeared throughout, may I say from a kid's perspective, I didn't want to know that many pages about anything. Thank you very much. And to think it was one of my major gifts that year. For me, the books were information overload. Good thing I also received a doll and ice skates.

One volume in the set, however, was a bonus book that I couldn't get enough of once I discovered it. It was an illustrated Bible. Not like the ones we have today. The black-and-white pictures were set up like a comic book, with captions under each frame. Without enticement, I read it repeatedly throughout my growing-up years and even into my young-adult life.

I guess *show me* was and is my easiest style of learning; it connects the dots between words and reasoning, which is probably why I love communicators who incorporate visual aids so I can see what they are saying.

Recently I met with a numbers specialist who went over

a chart of figures with me. After a few minutes, I could feel a rash breaking out on my midsection; then my eyes glazed over in confusion, and I slipped into a semi-stupor. When my forehead bounced off the table, he realized the conversation might be beyond me. Now, had he drawn little doodles and said, "These five puppies and these three hummingbirds equal this camel," I might have taken the journey with him. Nah, who am I kidding? I don't even think puppies could help my dog-eared brain, 'cause when you mention numerical facts, my cranial lobe becomes the Sahara in summer.

Jesus must have understood arid folks like me because He often spoke in wellspring stories, life-giving word pictures. I'm not that into *verily*s, *hath*s, or *thou*s, but take my hand with a story and lead me into truth, help me to picture instruction, and I'm there.

In the book of John, a story about a man appears. The fellow was sick for more than thirty-eight years, and he had been waiting by the pool of Bethesda for a miracle. From time to time, reportedly, an angel stirred the water at this pool. When he did, the first person in the pool would be healed of his or her sickness.

Okay, now, that's a story with a hook. We have human misery, a divine messenger, and a splinter of hope. I can see it, I can feel it, and I want to know what happens next. I can imagine scores of sick folks crowded around the pool and resting on the five porches nearby, seeking shade from the scorching sun. Many of the sick were carried there by family, all longing for the miraculous. Imagine if it were your loved one, how attentive you would be to the movement of the water, knowing only one would be healed at each stirring. It must have been a place of great groaning, sadness, and stench from unmedicated wounds and untreated diseases. Then an angel arrives, and suddenly a raucous race for first place blasts onto the scene. Like running with the bulls, people are pushing, clawing, cursing, falling, trying to be the one who wins.

Jesus arrives at the suffering scene and approaches the man who has been ill for so many years. But instead of instructing him on a health plan, Christ puts forth an unsettling query, "Do you want to be healed?"

How absurd. What a question. At face value it seems unnecessary. Why else would he be at the pool if he didn't want to be healed? It would have been easier for the sick man just to stay home and watch *Jeopardy*. The story tells us that the man had no one to lift him into the water. Family, friends, and neighbors probably had grown weary after that many years. It must have taken a great effort for him to even get there. Perhaps he paid out his last monies to have someone drop his aching body at the pool on his way to market. I'm sure every painful jostle of the journey he must have cried, "Lord, heal me!"

Or maybe after the passing of years, he was numb, too afraid to hope, and this was his last-ditch effort. Perhaps he thought that if this didn't work, he would just wither and die.

The inquiry, "Do you want to be healed?" seems insensitive to say to a man who had suffered for so long. Especially coming from Christ, the compassionate One.

Perhaps that question was like the one we ask a child when we are about to give her important information, and we want to gain her attention. We ask, "Are you listening to me?" Or maybe Christ was allowing the man to examine his own situation lest he had become so stuck in a rhythm of illness that he had closed the door to hope. There is a difference between resignation and relinquishment. Resignation says, "I quit." Relinquishment says, "I trust."

Whatever the reason for the question, Christ knows the man has inclined his heart because he hears and answers the Lord. It's at this point, after the question, that Jesus gives him seven words of clear instruction, "Rise, take up your bed and walk."

Just like that. We're told the man immediately was made whole. After all those years, he was well. Finally, fully well. Imagine, as he picks up his bed, how he must feel. Light as a feather, he moves through the people; he's hardly able to contain his joy. Tears cascade down his face. What a moment, what a miracle!

Now, there's a picture worth pondering.

Bits and Pieces

1. What is your learning style—aural or visual?
2. List the attributes of a good listener.
3. When was the last time you had to take instruction from someone?
4. What miraculous thing have you witnessed?
5. What stirs you?
6. In what area of your life do you need hope?
7. Do these words apply to you: "Rise, take up your bed and walk"? How?

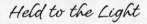

Held to the Light

Give ear, O my people, to my law; incline your ears to the words of my mouth. (Psalm 78:1)

For whatever things were written before were written for our learning, that we through the patience and comfort of the Scriptures might have hope. (Romans 15:4)

Now so it was that after three days they found Him in the temple, sitting in the midst of the teachers, both listening to them and asking them questions. And all who heard Him were astonished at His understanding and answers. (Luke 2:46–47)

Therefore I speak to them in parables. (Matthew 13:13a)

CHAPTER 19

Stretch Marks

If your enemy is hungry, give . . .

—PROVERBS 25:21

Huh? Give? Enemy?

Enemy and *give*? Do you really think God meant to put those two words in the same sentence? I mean, how unnatural is that? It's like peanut butter slathered over a meatloaf, sour milk in a smoothie, Tabasco sauce over a hot fudge sundae, or raw meat in a coconut cream pie. Okay, okay, I'll stop.

I get a kick out of giving to my children, grandchildren, and friends, but give to my enemies? C'mon, who deliberately does that? Well, okay, besides Jesus.

The heart of this proverb is that, if you see your enemy has a need, meet it. Now, here's my deal. Left to my own humanity, I'm not always nice to those whom I love; so how do you think I'd measure up with someone who is on my I-don't-think-so list?

Yes, I know, I know. I shouldn't have those kinds of lists . . . and I don't have a physical list. Mine is subtler and can surprise even me when it's highlighted. It's a low, grinding grudge, sort of like a car whose engine won't turn over.

I become aware of my list when a person on it succeeds, and resentment burbles to the surface, full of the stench of sulfur.* Or when someone snubs me and I want to trip her in response. Or when he says something that takes me back to the moment of the original offense between us, causing the old wound to fester.

And then God says, "Give."

------

* sulfur: a nonmetallic combustible used to make gunpowder

Have you ever noticed how doing things God's way adds stretch marks to our grace? I have. I mean, I have stretch marks. They are reminders that I expanded far enough to make space for my growing babies. I remember on one doctor's visit, after measuring my huge tummy, he asked, "How in the world can the body stretch that far?"

I thought he knew! I certainly couldn't answer that. I was having enough trouble just carrying my tonnage around. I tried not to take his incredulous stare personally . . . even though his eyebrows stayed stuck in his hairline for the rest of the exam. I gained thirty pounds with both my boys, and for my five-foot frame, that was a lot. I mean *a lot!* Think of a bin of watermelons. The elderly would hold open doors as I waddled and wedged my way through.

Here's what struck me about this verse on enemies and giving and how baby stretch marks and grace fit in—I really do have a point.

The baby marks are created when the infant puts pressure against the mom's belly and the skin stretches to make more room. That's what grace does—it makes space not only for birthing a baby but also for the more difficult task of accepting our enemies . . . so we don't shoot them. Grace makes space for imperfections without retaliation. Grace resolves I-don't-think-so lists so we can move on. Yes, there will be some aggressive enemies who will press hard on grace, causing it to stretch thin to make room to contain them. But somehow grace does it . . . because grace gives and gives and gives . . . stretches and stretches and stretches . . . even when it's undeserved. Otherwise, we who were once God's enemies would still be hostile toward Him. But because of the grace-space

Jesus made for us when He died on Calvary, we stand in His presence forgiven . . . and qualified to give to others, even those who offend us.

I'm grateful I haven't been left to my own self-absorbed responses. Aren't you? Had it not been for God's intervention, just think of the debris we could have left in our path. Not to mention a few scalps, scathing comments, and multiple abrasions and contusions.

Abraham Lincoln observed, "The best way to destroy an enemy is to make him a friend." I find that for me to be a true giver to my enemies, I must stay current with the One who continues to rescue me from my tendencies, which seem to be Fed-Exed to me daily. I must keep short accounts with the Lord and others so things don't pile up on my doorstep.

Bits and Pieces

1. In what ways are you a giver?
2. Who is on your I-don't-think-so list?
3. How many festering wounds do you have?
4. What does resentment feel like?
5. Read Proverbs 25:21, 22 and answer these questions: What two things does God ask us to give to our enemies? And what is our payoff at the end of verse 22?
6. When has your grace had to stretch the most?
7. How can you keep short accounts with God? With others?
8. What's piling up on your doorstep?
9. What do you do to keep short accounts?
10. How do you make an enemy a friend?

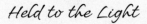

Held to the Light

For the LORD God is a sun and shield; the LORD will give grace . . . no good thing will He withhold from those who walk uprightly. (Psalm 84:11)

You prepare a table before me in the presence of my enemies. (Psalm 23:5a)

"'You shall love the LORD your God with all your heart, with all your soul, and with all your mind.' This is the first and great commandment. And the second is like it: 'You shall love your neighbor as yourself.'" (Matthew 22:37–39)

And now for a little while grace has been shown from the LORD our God, to leave us a remnant to escape, and to give us a peg in His holy place, that our God may enlighten our eyes and give us a measure of revival in our bondage. (Ezra 9:8)

And whenever you stand praying, if you have anything against anyone, forgive him, that your Father in heaven may also forgive you your trespasses. (Mark 11:25)

Do not rejoice when your enemy falls, and do not let your heart be glad when he stumbles. (Proverbs 24:17)

CHAPTER 20

Anxiety Alert

Anxiety in the heart . . . causes depression.

—PROVERBS 12:25*a*

I could have been the poster child for this verse. Ms. Anxiety herself *unless* there was a swimsuit competition, then not so much: I have nervous ankles, quaking thighs, jiggly arms, and a Jell-O midsection. But anxiety alone? I was really good at that. I could whip up a batch of concern over almost anything.

A cloud in the sky meant a dangerous storm was about to descend on us, or at least me, and twirl us away. An unexplained glance from someone meant she despised me. A simple rash meant a deadly disease. A ride in a car meant an accident was imminent. A knock on the door represented a direct threat. A headache was a tumor, and a compliment was suspect.

Unfortunately I could go on and on. There was no end to how I could take almost any life experience and dip it into nerve-racking scrutiny, which eventually painted me into the corner of agoraphobia. Anxiety, while scary, comes with adrenaline rushes, which can be addictive but almost always end in depression. The body wasn't meant to be constantly on full alert.

Anxiety is the habit of fear that can end up controlling our lives. The good thing about habits is they can be broken. Not easily. But definitely. We are habitual creatures, and once we get into a routine, it takes focused effort and sometimes outside help to reestablish healthier behavior.

It took me time to realize that my anxiety was mine. Fear takes refuge in excuses. I kept thinking if things were different, I wouldn't be this way. If my husband were different, if we didn't have bills, if my health were stronger, if society were safer, if I had had different parents, if I lived somewhere else, if people were nicer . . . blah, blah, blah. It would be years before I recognized I was in charge of my anxiety, and with God's help I could change the quality of my existence.

I also became aware that my lifestyle supported my anxiety. I indulged my congested emotions with sad movies; I would listen to the same threatening news and/or weather broadcasts over and over; I would call everyone I knew to talk up a problem; I resisted change; I didn't eat well; I stewed over the past; I didn't exercise; and I slept way too much.

One morning I woke up and realized I was almost nonfunctional. I didn't want to get out of bed, bathe, dress, or take care of my family. On that eye-opening day, I made a decision . . . that I wanted to live.

The decision for life was huge. My journey didn't become easy; in some ways it initially became harder, but with the hourly choice to move forward, things began to shift.

With much prayer and strenuous effort, I gradually replaced negative life patterns. I got up earlier, which—trust me—wasn't natural. Even though I was cranky, I was up. Then I had to learn how to be pleasant. Okay, tolerable. It would take years before I became a rise-and-shine girl. But my first step was to move my muscles, regardless of how reluctant and rebellious they were, and get into a standing position. God designed our bodies to obey us, which means we can command our muscles to move and they will. At first it's a wrestling match, but with time it becomes more of a natural response. I find it helps if you say it aloud: "Move, feet, move!" People stare, but hey, they forget.

The strange thing about depression is that we often don't know we're depressed until someone else helps us see it. The symptoms are obvious, even glaring, especially to those around us, but because we think the way we are is about outside pressures instead of inside pressures, we don't see it for what it is. I knew I was sad, but I thought if everyone else would shape up, I'd be okay.

I'm not a doctor or a counselor, and everyone's journey has its own twists and turns, but I can tell you about my experience with depression. It was heavy, like trying to drag a leaded suit of armor everywhere I went. It was hard to press my way through brain fog, old voices, unwarranted exhaustion, defense mechanisms, shame, anger, self-pity, and hormonal havoc.

Becoming mentally sound and emotionally steady is wrenching work. And big changes usually require assistance. Help may come in the form of medication, counseling, support groups, doctors, or hospitalization. Perhaps all of the above. Whatever is needed to accomplish the change and to experience breakthroughs is worth it.

One of my fiercest battles was with my own thought-life. I had to develop a strategic plan to win over my taunting thoughts of misery and judgment. I searched the Scriptures and memorized uplifting verses. I joined a Bible study, and I read heart-cheering, faith-anchoring books that inspired me. And I still do.

Also, I watched people who were productive and happy and took notes on their lives. I needed physical examples of healthier behavior. From them I learned to tap the wealth found in humor, the restoration of solitude, and the mental and emotional benefits of creating, whether music, gardening, writing, designing, painting, or cooking. And I learned the healing benefits of shaking the scary contents of my heart out into the open so they could be aired and examined in the light.

Ah, the light. What a revelatory healer it is.

Bits and Pieces

1. Describe anxiety.
2. In what ways are you given to exaggeration?
3. What habits have you successfully broken?
4. What excuses do you make for unhealthy habits?
5. What lifestyle changes would it help you to make?
6. What emotional indulgences do you participate in?
7. Do you think you are depressed? Do others?
8. What condition is your thought life in?
9. Who do you take notes on because they seem to live life well?
10. When was the last time you aired your heart?

Held to the Light

And the LORD, He is the One who goes before you. He will be with you, He will not leave you nor forsake you; do not fear nor be dismayed. (Deuteronomy 31:8)

Fear not, for I am with you; be not dismayed, for I am your God. I will strengthen you, yes, I will help you, I will uphold you with My righteous right hand. (Isaiah 41:10)

For God has not given us a spirit of fear, but of power and of love and of a sound mind. (2 Timothy 1:7)

Consider the ravens, for they neither sow nor reap, which have neither storehouse nor barn; and God feeds them. Of how much more value are you than the birds? (Luke 12:24)

If we live in the Spirit, let us also walk in the Spirit. (Galatians 5:25)

When my soul fainted within me, I remembered the LORD; and my prayer went up to You, into Your holy temple. (Jonah 2:7)

And whatever things you ask in prayer, believing, you will receive. (Matthew 21:22)

Therefore you shall lay up these words of mine in your heart and in your soul. (Deuteronomy 11:18a)

CHAPTER 21

Loose Lips

The heart of the wise teaches his mouth,
and adds learning to his lips.

—PROVERBS 16:23

"*Okay, lips, listen up.* You know that tone you used with the cashier? Not necessary. And the sarcasm that slipped from you with your husband when all he did was suggest you watch your spending . . . tsk-tsk. Then there's the tidbit of information you shared that wasn't yours to tell. What's that about, Ms. Lippy?"

Teach your mouth. I love that concept. I'm told in the book of James that I can't control my tongue, but according to this proverb, I can teach it a thing or two. Perhaps the more we instruct our mouths, the fewer things we will say that we regret? Whoa, that would be so worth it.

Do you love learning new things? I do. And I love telling what I learned. For instance, did you know that if you wipe a sheet of fabric softener on yourself before walking outside, it will keep mosquitoes away? Who knew? Dried candle wax on carpeting lifts off when you place a cloth on it and iron over the cloth. I've used that tip more than once. And if you're too chilly to climb between cold sheets on a winter's night, heat them up with warm drafts of air from your blow dryer.

Aren't those fun facts? Yet I know this proverb isn't suggesting we focus on household trivia but that we get a grip on life-changing truth. So I've listed a few eclectic things that I'm still learning. I recommend that you pause on each statement and ask yourself, "Is this true?" If so, "How have I experienced this truth?" And finally, "Are my actions and my words in agreement?"

- Loving the Lord with all our hearts, souls, minds, and strength is easier than continually living with the regret and rubble of having done things our way.
- Pride is the helium of an inflated ego.
- Words have the power to wither the human spirit.
- Arrogance is a cover for shame.
- Joy is highly contagious.
- Anger is high-octane fuel for fear.
- We can be brave while our knees are knocking.
- Self-pity implodes dignity.
- Our mind can override our emotions.
- We are our finest selves when we function in our God-given gifts.
- Friends mirror our reflection.
- People who disagree with us could bring a fresh perspective.
- Staying stuck is a choice.
- Apologizing buffs out mars in our integrity.
- We tend to express our safest emotions.
- Change keeps us on the cusp of growth.
- Creation never stops expounding on God.
- Friends are a necessary part of sanity.
- We never outgrow our fallibility.
- Humor isn't funny if it's at someone else's expense. No . . . matter . . . who . . . laughs.
- Limitations are not necessarily deficiencies.
- Love must be spoken.
- Our anger reveals more about us than others. (Oh, shoot!)
- Fear crouches in the dark cave of what-ifs, stirring embers.

When what slips through our lips is good, true, pure, just, lovely, and of good report, then we will be following the counsel of this proverb. Try this: consciously listen to your words over the next day; take notes if necessary. You may be surprised what's slipping out your lips. I was.

Bits and Pieces

1. List the ways wisdom impacts words.
2. What are you doing to teach your lips?
3. Who do you know who exemplifies wisdom by her words?
4. What words withered your spirit? What have you done to recover?
5. When were you knee-knocking brave?
6. How have friends helped you *see* yourself?
7. How do you express your love verbally?
8. At what point can we stop teaching our lips?
9. Select five statements from the list in this chapter, and journal your feelings.

Held to the Light

The lips of the wise disperse knowledge, but the heart of the fool does not do so. (Proverbs 15:7)

A wise man will hear and increase learning, and a man of understanding will attain wise counsel. (Proverbs 1:5)

For the LORD gives wisdom; from His mouth come knowledge and understanding. (Proverbs 2:6)

Finally, brethren, whatever things are true, whatever things are noble, whatever things are just, whatever things are pure, whatever things are lovely, whatever things are of good report, if there is any virtue and if there is anything praiseworthy— meditate on these things. (Philippians 4:8)

Now therefore, go, and I will be with your mouth and teach you what you shall say. (Exodus 4:12)

Restore to me the joy of Your salvation, and uphold me by Your generous Spirit. (Psalm 51:12)

CHAPTER 22

Looking Up

His secret counsel is with the upright.

—PROVERBS 3:32*b*

God telling us His secret counsel? What an honor!

Ah, but wait. There are stipulations on whom He reveals His secret counsel to. It's reserved for those who are upright. *Hmm. Upright* isn't a word we hear much these days. Wonder why?

Let's see; it means "honorable, honest, just."

Oh, maybe that's why.

Those qualities don't fit easily into our instant-winner, flash-in-the-pan, multitasking lifestyles. But here's the thing about upright—it can add inches to our height and steel to our backbone, making it well worth our consideration and time.

A story in the Bible that deeply moves me is the one about a woman who couldn't stand upright. Because I have osteo issues with my aging bones, I have empathy for this gal. And while I feel bad that I'm losing inches, this poor dear was bent over almost in half. She had been staring at the fissured earth and the frayed sandals of passersby for eighteen years.

Eighteen years!

Imagine for a moment what that must have felt like to be unable to toss back your head and fill the air with laughter, or look into your loved ones' eyes, or watch a bird soar over a mountain peak, or even peer down the path ahead. She couldn't stretch up high enough to drop her bucket in the well, or reach a cup on a shelf, or hang her sorrow on a hook. Her world was filled with kicked-up dust, gritty feet, barking dogs, and the taunts of rowdy children, who more than once toppled her for sport. I'm sure she was often dismissed, overlooked, and underestimated.

Yet when Jesus saw her, He called her to Himself. Her moment had come. Finally she was noticed, preferred, considered. How different that must have felt to her neglected spirit. What a stunning moment when, over all others, the Messiah favored her.

Imagine . . . to be seen, to be called out, to be touched by the Savior. After eighteen years of being bowed. I wonder, as she made her way to Jesus, straining to see her next step, following His voice, accepting His invitation, if her heart didn't palpitate with hope.

Then Christ did the unthinkable . . .

And He laid His hands on her, and immediately she was made straight, and glorified God. (Luke 13:13)

You would think the church folks would have thrown a potluck dinner and roasted a lamb, having just witnessed such a miracle. They knew this woman. She had been in their midst for years, curled over and stumbling between them. But now she stood straight; she leaped and danced. The leaders saw full-on her grateful face. They looked into her amazed eyes and heard her thankful heart.

Yet festivities were not the order of the day. No roasted lamb, no deviled eggs, no strawberry shortcake—because Christ had the audacity to heal this woman on the Sabbath. He broke a law to perform a divine act of love and reveal to all of them a new liberty, and they, instead of celebrating, were bent over in withered disgust.

I ask you: Who was more disabled—the lady who responded without hesitation to Christ's voice or the religious leaders who were halted by their legalism?

Many heard Christ's words, but only the woman responded to the message, "You are loosed." There were obviously others who needed to be shaken loose from their arrogance, their ruts, their shortsightedness. But only the woman rose up to her full intended stature and praised God. Because that's what the upright of heart do . . . they live in the liberty of God's counsel.

The leaders heard what Christ said; they were standing a heartbeat away, but they didn't get it. They saw the woman change from crippled to whole, and they still missed it. How could that be? The secret counsel was only unlocked in the hearts of those who came with an ear to hear.

I think that woman probably was of greater stature when she was bent in half than those leaders were standing erect in their judgmental robes and haughty beards. So smug. So certain. So missing the point.

I've been judgmental. I've preferred a law over a sister's need for mercy more than once. I've gathered my robes around me and missed the point of grace more than once. When I was brought low by my own haughty heart, Christ, in His mercy, loosed me more than once.

Some days I stand taller than others. How about you?

And some days I'm the crumpled woman, bent over in my need and unable to do anything about it—feeling unheard and, at times, unnecessary, longing to walk upright.

During those times especially, I wait to hear God's secret counsel for me.

Bits and Pieces

1. What secrets has God revealed to you?
2. What sorrow(s) have you carried for many years?
3. When did you feel you weren't seen?
4. When were you dismissed? Overlooked? Underestimated?
5. List your disabilities.
6. When has your heart ricocheted with hope?
7. What does it mean to have "ears to hear"?
8. When were you judgmental?
9. In what areas of your life have you accepted Christ's invitation to be loosed?

Held to the Light

Surely the righteous shall give thanks to Your name; the upright shall dwell in Your presence. (Psalm 140:13)

Let integrity and uprightness preserve me, for I wait for You. (Psalm 25:21)

Do good, O LORD, to those who are good, and to those who are upright in their hearts. (Psalm 125:4)

His delight is in the fear of the LORD, and he shall not judge by the sight of His eyes, nor decide by the hearing of His ears. (Isaiah 11:3).

Judge not, and you shall not be judged. Condemn not, and you shall not be condemned. Forgive, and you will be forgiven. (Luke 6:37)

For the LORD God is a sun and shield: the LORD will give grace and glory; no good thing will He withhold from those who walk uprightly. (Psalm 84:11)

CHAPTER 23

Buggy

*There are four things which are little on the earth,
but they are exceedingly wise.*

—PROVERBS 30:24

I don't do bugs. At least, not well. Some folks are fascinated by them but not me. I basically try to stay out of their way. I'm crazy about fireflies but only when they are outside, showing off. As a kid, I did think it might be fun to have an ant farm, which meant the ants were contained, and I could watch them excavate. But ants are so busy all the time that I was afraid, even though they couldn't get out of their glass enclosure, that I would feel crawly. So I nixed that idea and stayed with dolls, cutouts, and baseball.

I took this "I don't do bugs" philosophy with me right into adulthood. So one day, when I noticed a couple of big ants in my kitchen cupboard among the canned goods, I was irritated. I wasn't afraid to dispose of them, but I found it troublesome that they knew my address. I pulled all the cans out of the cupboard and did a thorough search, but I didn't find any more.

Over the next few days I noticed an ant in my bathroom, followed by two in my home office. I mentioned it to my husband, who grew up in the wildwoods of northern Michigan, where it was common to have bears and deer sit down in your living room and chug back a beer; so he couldn't imagine anyone being dismayed over an occasional, itty-bitty ant.

One night after we had gone to bed, Les was softly snoring . . . okay, he was buzz-sawing a forest, and I was reading myself to sleep when something bit me. Yes, bit me. I jumped out of that bed so abruptly I scared the sleep right out of Les.

He sat up, flailing. "What's wrong? What's wrong?"

"Something bit me." I checked for teeth marks and blood

on my leg and instead found a pencil-point red dot. (Hysteria runs in my ancestry.)

"What do you mean?" he said, trying to shake the fresh cobwebs out of his head.

"What does a person usually mean when they say they've been bit?" I responded, aggravated that he wasn't fire-hosing the premises, loading his rifle, summoning the military, or taking some other kind of reasonable measure to protect me.

Les threw back the covers, and there it was, strutting across the sheets—a big, fat, solitary, black ant. I thought the critter looked smug. Well, Les wiped that smile off that ant's face fast, and then we (I) inspected every square inch of the bedding, in case the bug had a friend in tow. Even though the bed appeared to be insect free, I jumped awake off and on throughout the night. By morning Les announced he was calling an exterminator for his own sanity.

When the bug man arrived, I pointed to the kitchen cupboard first, but as he visually scanned the area, he seemed uninterested. Then he asked permission to walk around the house, which I gave him. In less than five minutes he had found the source of our problem. To our surprise he guided Les and me into our bedroom and pointed to our bedroom door. We stared at him.

He said, "Listen." He motioned us to place our ears against the wood.

We leaned in, and we could hear a hum of scratching movement.

I jumped back, and the man said, "You have thousands of ants in there."

Then he said, "Look." He pointed to the floor where a

stream of ants, like a strand of black beads, was coming out of the vent, across the baseboard, and under the door, where they then disappeared into the interior of the door.

He explained that a colony had set up ant-life inside our door and was using the venting system like a superhighway to access every room in the house. I was aghast. To think, thousands of them were within three feet of my bed. We were lucky in the night that they didn't pick up our bed and evict us. I thought, too bad we couldn't put a glass on the door. Then we could sit in bed and watch our very own kaleidoscope of ants. Not.

My husband and the bug guy removed the door from the premises, and then the exterminator sprayed the house for any strays.

I had my own ant farm and didn't even know it. All I was missing were the cows and horses. I still think it's a miracle that something so small can take on such ambitious tasks with such tenacity, not to mention their architectural skill. And their work force was amazingly harmonious and strategic.

Because of that firsthand experience, which repeated itself at the next country home we lived in, I gained an appreciation for an ant's tireless approach to life. And I wasn't surprised to find that ants were the first example in the list in Proverbs of creatures who are small yet wise. It goes on to tell us, "The ants are a people not strong, yet they prepare their food in the summer" (Proverbs 30:25).

So that's what they were doing in my cupboard. Golly, the ant in my bed must have thought he hit the mother lode when he tried to take a chunk out of me. Probably thought I was the supersize company picnic. I'm just glad he didn't have time to call for backup.

Bits and Pieces

1. What bugs you?
2. What childhood philosophy have you taken into adulthood?
3. Who do you wish didn't have your address? Why?
4. What attribute runs in your ancestry?
5. What do you need for your sanity?
6. What was the last ambitious task you tackled?
7. What makes your work environment harmonious? Unharmonious?
8. How do you demonstrate a tireless approach to life?

Held to the Light

Then Solomon determined to build a temple for the name of the LORD. (2 Chronicles 2:1a)

Let nothing be done through selfish ambition or conceit, but in lowliness of mind let each esteem others better than himself. (Philippians 2:3)

Be strong and of good courage, do not fear nor be afraid of them; for the LORD your God, He is the One who goes with you. He will not leave you nor forsake you. (Deuteronomy 31:6)

Therefore strengthen the hands which hang down, and the feeble knees, and make straight paths for your feet. (Hebrews 12:12–13a)

*Oh, magnify the L*ORD *with me, and let us exalt His name together. (Psalm 34:3).*

And the men did the work faithfully. (2 Chronicles 34:12a)

. . . .

CHAPTER 24

Sewing Kit for the Heart

Who can find a virtuous wife?

—PROVERBS 31:10*a*

I say for those in pursuit of a virtuous wife, try eBay; I hear they have rare finds. Don't get me wrong—I know many admirable women, but I must say, none measures up to the list of all perfectionist lists found in Proverbs 31.

I don't know how you feel about the Proverbs 31 woman, but honestly, she supersizes my guilt meter. She's so, so, well, perfect while I'm just, uh, so-so.

Recently a seminary graduate told me the Proverbs lady isn't real but instead a composite picture of who every mom hopes her son marries and what every woman would like to become. Phew! Wish I'd known that sooner.

I find that comparing either helps us lift our banners higher or causes us to give up and cry defeat. We all need examples, so the tricky part is not losing sight of our unique design. We don't want to fall down the "we are not enough" bottomless pit.

For instance, it took me years of sewing pant legs together, buttons offset of the holes, and ski-sloping hemlines to real-ize that, no matter how much I practiced, sewing wasn't my forte; it would not become my profession; and it was better left to others. I won't even admit to how many times I sewed myself to an item. It scares my husband when I take out a needle and head in the direction of the mend pile. He leaps up, sprints past me, with arms flailing, calling out, "I'll do it! I'll do it!"

But if you're trying to mend, say, a broken heart, I may be of some help. Because of the extent of my own brokenness, I recognize the threads that can whipstitch your dignity back in place, tack up your perspective a tad higher, and help cross-stitch some hope securely back onto your faith. God has given me access to the sewing kit of hearts to the degree I have been mended myself . . . and while I continue to make regular visits to my Tailor for my own ongoing repairs, I'm grateful for the prowess in sewing He has taught me thus far in areas I never expected.

Our Proverbs gal is said to have been one who worked willingly with her hands, which immediately reminded me of my mom. She could do anything. Mom could landscape a yard, reupholster a chair, reroof a shed, transform a house into a home, crochet tablecloths, and make meals that caused folks to line up at her door.

Me . . . not so much. Folks at my place are lining up to get out. Oh, sure I can do all of those things, and I do, but it's obvious I do them like a kindergartner's art project. As far as my cooking, my family is relieved if they can identify my offerings. I so love the unexpected. They so enjoy the predictable. I still have trouble making the components of the meal come out at the same time. Somehow nobody appreciates cooked carrots served with their chocolate éclairs.

Ah, but I have the potential to cook up a fun message, a tasty story, or a seasoned tale that may tickle your palate. I love to brew words until they cause a teakettle to whistle, a pot to bubble over, or a toaster to pop. Like morsels of food, words can fill us up until we have to unhook our britches and burp (excuse me) with relief.

There are many ways God chooses and uses the abilities and gifts of His people. When we stop grieving what we are not and start living what we are, I find that not only does a satisfaction in our offerings arise, but the world also becomes a friendlier place to live in. It's easier to fill our slot on the planet that contributes to others.

Another benefit of finding the best ways to express our God-given design is that it frees us to celebrate others' gifts without feeling less-than or sinking into the treacherous muck of jealousy or resentment.

Of course, we must guard against complacency and always be willing to try a new area. There may be an undercover gift lurking whose time has come. Remember Grandma Moses? She was a widow and mother of ten children (five died in infancy). Her gift for art didn't emerge until she was in her seventies when she sold her work in drugstores. Eventually she became one of the most popular painters of the twentieth century. She worked willingly with her hands.

I thank God for the woman who hems my pants with expertise and for my husband who sews on a button with absolute precision. I admire their artistry. I'm grateful, too, for a mom who was as diverse in her abilities as the patterns in a kaleidoscope and who left detailed touches as her legacy.

It was from her I learned how to clean a house, set a table, appreciate antiques, create an inviting bed, greet a guest, make a plateful of yummy deviled eggs, and follow the Lord.

So while my table will be set with creativity, and grace may be stirring, you might want to bring take-out as a backup. If I were you, I'd bring something that goes with eggs. Know what I mean?

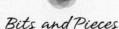

Bits and Pieces

1. What are your thoughts on the Proverbs 31 woman?
2. How does comparison feel?
3. What can you mend?
4. What does "working willingly" mean to you?
5. What do you like to cook up?
6. What gifts do you admire in others?
7. What gift do you have that surprised you?
8. When was the last time you felt jealous of someone else's gift?
9. List some of the good things you learned from your mother.

Held to the Light

A time to tear, and a time to sew. (Ecclesiastes 3:7a)

For I long to see you, that I may impart to you some spiritual gift, so that you may be established. (Romans 1:11)

A gracious woman retains honor. (Proverbs 11:16a)

Commit your works to the LORD. (Proverbs 16:3a)

Let them do good, that they may be rich in good works, ready to give, willing to share. (1 Timothy 6:18)

CHAPTER 25

Trapped

The fear of man brings a snare.

—PROVERBS 29:25*a*

It's hard not to fear some people, don't you think? Like an employer, who holds your finances in his hand; or your mate, who might decide to ditch you; or your children, who could withdraw their love or your grandchildren. That's all scary stuff.

Yet we know ultimately that God makes provision and position for us. And if our mates left, we're promised a husband in Christ, and even if our children forsake us, God never will. Mentally I hear that. Yet . . .

I still think people are scary, which isn't good because then I give them power over me that they were never meant to have. I assign them the position of determining the quality of my future. Now, that's really scary, which I'm sure is why this verse warns us that fearing people traps us.

Let's talk traps for a minute. As a boy, my husband—along with his dad and brothers—trapped animals for their hides, and sometimes for food as well. Those of you who are animal rights activists, you might want to skip this section, which I was thinking of doing myself, but I really want to fully grasp this verse.

In the northern woods of the Upper Peninsula of Michigan, life was hard, work was scarce, and the winters were severe, averaging more than 360 inches of snow per year. Eight people were in Les's family, so they had to be creative year-round just to put food on the table. The children were all enlisted in this endeavor. They would sell catalog seeds to neighbors, and with the money they made, their dad would buy seeds for their eighty-by-fifty-foot garden that he planted. The children helped tend the garden as well as harvest the produce. Then their mom would can it. She not only canned the fruit and vegetables but also the meat that they trapped.

They would set traps on the water's edge or in the woods and then cover them with grass and twigs. Watching to see where the animal runs were (worn tracks going back and forth), they placed the steel traps accordingly. Beaver, mink, rabbit, and weasels were caught.

Okay, back to fearing people. I do believe this kind of fear is set in place by the enemy of our souls. I think he watches for our runs, our life patterns, and when he finds our watering hole, he lays the fear-of-people steel trap, knowing the grip it will have on us.

The proverb for this chapter is meant to keep us out of the snare, but if you're like I am, you don't really understand the implications until after the trap has snapped shut and we're dragging the weight of it wherever we go.

Early in my marriage, I found myself in the trap of intimidation. My hubby was emotionally threatening. That's a hard sentence for me to write because I adore this man, and I know it doesn't portray his heart, just his damage. Even in those years of angry outbursts, it was easy to overlook because most of the time he was so jovial, kind, and generous. But when something set him off, his response was like dynamite exploding.

The thing I found most frightening was when he would suggest that he planned to leave me. I couldn't stand the thought of that kind of abandonment. It took years before I realized I was stuck in a snare, and we as a family were living in a scary cycle. I knew I needed to address Les's behavior and that we needed to find healthier and safer ways to communicate.

Finally I realized that I would have to risk Les's leaving me to restore safety in my home and to recover my own dignity. Here's the amazing thing: When I faced what I feared, I heard the clank of the steel trap open, and I stepped out . . . but not without a limp. We still had much to work out between us because you don't get that stuck without both parties participating.

When I look back, I'm stunned that Les had those harsh spells because he is so tenderhearted. His father was a dangerous abuser, resulting in Les needing to be coached in finding a better way to handle his feelings and pain. I'm grateful that, unlike his father, Les was willing to go for counseling and to make changes. He, too, was caught in a snare of intimidation, one his father set for him and his siblings long ago, where life was hard, work was scarce, and winters were severe.

People are scary often because we let them be. But most certainly, if we don't break the cycle of fear we experience around those folks, they are empowered in ways that trap us in a life we don't want. God can give us the strength to break free. It's not easy, but we don't have to remain trapped.

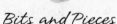

Bits and Pieces

1. Whom do you fear and why?
2. What happens when other people have power over us?
3. Have you ever been trapped? Explain.
4. What has a grip on you?
5. Define *intimidation*.

6. Who intimidates you? Why?

7. Do you fear abandonment?

8. How does one create a safe environment?

9. What kind of harsh spells do you have?

Held to the Light

The LORD is my light and my salvation; whom shall I fear?
The LORD is the strength of my life; of whom shall I be afraid?
(Psalm 27:1)

There is no fear in love; but perfect love casts out fear, because
fear involves torment. (1 John 4:18a)

[God] delivered me from my strong enemy, from those who
hated me, for they were too strong for me. They confronted
me in the day of my calamity, but the LORD was my support.
He also brought me out into a broad place; He delivered me
because He delighted in me. (Psalm 18:17–19)

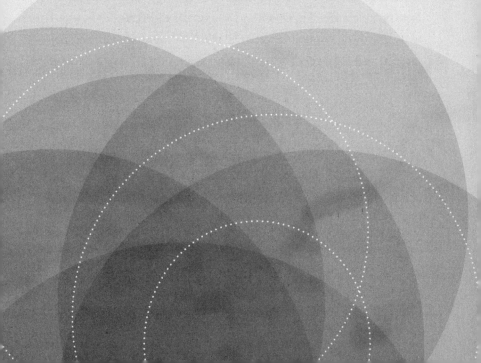

CHAPTER 26

Lost . . . and Found

*Ponder the path of your feet, and let all
your ways be established.*

—PROVERBS 4:26

I'm directionally impaired. Somebody unplugged my GPS. Not the electronic one, my internal one. I have no natural compass. And here's the part that bugs me: I keep proving it.

Not long ago I was at a hotel that was two and a half blocks away from my favorite department store chain. I was in need—okay, I was in want—of several things, and the weather was great. So I decided to mosey over. Now, granted, the walk was at a couple of odd angles, and some construction had to be maneuvered around, but from the hotel the store was spitting distance . . . if one were given to such sport.

I spent a couple of hours just poking around the store and then headed back. At least that was my intention. When I reached the first corner, I crossed at the light and stepped up on the sidewalk. That's when I realized I didn't know where I was. Nothing looked familiar. I tried to mentally retrace my arrival and then reverse it but to no avail. I don't have a backup shifter in my brain.

Finally, I asked a pedestrian if he knew where such-and-such hotel was. An odd look crossed over his face. I think he was trying to decide if I was serious or if we were on some silly video game. Then he smirked and pointed behind me to two skyscraping towers and said, "It's right there."

I laughed nervously and quipped, "Guess I should have dropped breadcrumbs," and then I turned and skittered toward the tallest buildings within miles.

Now, while that's not a hopelessly lost story, the hopeless

part came the next day. I returned to that same store to pick up
slacks I had asked to be altered, only to end up on the same corner, lost again. I know, I know; that's pitiful. Talk about walking
in circles. I stood there on that corner and thought, *Now, was
I supposed to turn right out of that door instead of left?* Once
again nothing looked familiar. Yikes!

I stopped another walker and inquired as to the location
of my hotel, and he pointed over my head and said, "Lady, it's
right behind you," in a tone that suggested I might have escaped
from the home. I turned, and sure enough, there stood the two
towers in the same place I'd left them, beckoning me home. I
wanted to spit.

My directionally gifted husband is stunned and I think
impressed by my consistency. At least that's my read on his
eye-rolling, head-wagging response, like I might be a lot to
take in. He is the type who can go somewhere once and twenty
years later remember how to get back there. I find that annoy-
ing yet comforting in light of my loopy design.

Obviously before I had set out for the store I hadn't "pon-
dered the path of my feet." Instead, I took in the traffic, the way
pedestrians were dressed, and the city sounds. So when it was
time to go back, I had no landmarks. Everything I had focused
on had changed.

It's wise to stop every once in a while and ask ourselves,
"Where am I?" and "Where am I going?" It helps us realign our
compasses.

Two friends were caught up in a conversation and hardly
noticed when a third gentleman joined them. Though they
were aware of an extra set of sandals stirring up dust as they
walked, their reliving of the dramatic days prior held their

attention. Then the new man posed a question, which startled the men out of their conversation and caused them to wonder where this stranger had been that he was so uninformed of recent events. They began to bring him up to speed, or so they thought, but when they took a breath, the man helped them to understand the real truth of what had transpired. After arriving at their village, the men begged the intriguing wayfarer to stay. During dinner, after the bread had been blessed and broken, the two friends had a revelation, an eye-opening moment, and realized they were with Jesus.

Those men weren't lost; they knew the path home, but they were so distracted and off course in their own surmising of life that they didn't recognize the risen Savior walking with them. After their *aha* moment, Jesus disappeared. The one then turned to the other and questioned . . .

"Did not our heart burn within us while He talked with us on the road, and while He opened the Scriptures to us?" (Luke 24:32*b*).

There it is, our GPS, our navigational system: Jesus walks with us, and His Word establishes our path. We just need aha moments when our eyes are opened to His presence, and then we need to receive the Word until it burns within us.

Would that have helped me the day I stood at the street corner of Lost? Now that I think about it, I actually did all the right things: I stopped to ask, "Where am I? Where am I going?"

Have you checked your bearings lately?

Bits and Pieces

1. On a scale of 1 to 10, with 10 being the highest, rate your natural compass, your intuitive sense of placement.
2. When was the last time you were turned around?
3. When was the last time you asked for directions? How hard was it to decide you needed help?
4. When have you felt hopeless?
5. When have you felt you were walking in circles?
6. Do you know where you are? Do you know where you're going?
7. What did you learn from your last eye-opening experience?
8. When did your heart burn with revelation?
9. Have you ever stood at the street corner of Lost?

Held to the Light

He leads me in the paths of righteousness for His name's sake. (Psalm 23:3b)

Blessed is the man who walks not in the counsel of the ungodly, nor stands in the path of sinners, nor sits in the seat of the scornful. (Psalm 1:1)

That you may walk worthy of the Lord, fully pleasing Him, being fruitful in every good work and increasing in the knowledge of God. (Colossians 1:10)

Your ears shall hear a word behind you, saying, "This is the way, walk in it." (Isaiah 30:21)

For the ways of man are before the eyes of the LORD, and He ponders all His paths. (Proverbs 5:21)

CHAPTER 27

In the Beginning

Who has gathered the wind in His fists?

—PROVERBS 30:4*a*

Don't you love this question? What a picture! Artists, grab your paintbrushes!

I love visual verses. In fact, I've been a fan of "in the beginning," well, since the genesis of my walk with the Lord. I love imagining the creation moments when the Spirit of God hovered over the waters and gathered the wind in His fists.

What do you think the beginning of creation looked like? Not that we could do it justice, but it's thrilling to stretch the canvas of our minds.

My thoughts turn to visions of exploding light and swirling waters. Mountains rising up with great groans and creaking as they settle into place. Valleys dipping down, playing with streams and bursting forth with flowers. Birds filling the air with ancient hymns as the winged creatures seek out great woods and deep forests. An enormous fiery ball, rolling across the horizon and nesting into its appointed path while multitudes of stars twirl at lightning speed in a flurry of directions.

Oh, to have been a speckled frog on a lily pad. Talk about a light show with water features. Hello!

Here's what I don't get when I consider that my God holds the winds in His fist and spoke the world into existence: Why, oh, why, do I worry? Fret? Or fear?

In the beginning, when I had my first panic attack, my life-orbit stopped, and gripping panic set me on a scary path—a path full of exploding fear and swirling insecurity. My mountainous mood swings sent me plunging into the valley of depression. For several years I shuffled, lost in the deep forest of guilt and regret. My fiery anger nested and grew inside of me and struck at others with lightning-bolt speed. I was miserable in my new, dark world.

So how does one find the light of day again? For me, the path was long and rocky and filled with hard work. God didn't speak my healing into being. He didn't make it easy or fast. No shortcuts. The winds of adversity continued to swirl on my path. And I'm grateful. Now. It cost me a lot in years and tears, but I learned out of desperation things I'm sure I would never have known otherwise. These insights help me today to share in meaningful ways with others who are where I was.

Do I believe God put me through emotional and mental struggles for the purpose of making me stronger? I do not. We live in a broken world tainted with sin. Sin robs us of our dignity, but God in His mercy rescues us. I believe the Lord redeemed my damage to use it for good. That is His heart.

I'm often asked how I got well, how I went from housebound to airborne. I always hesitate before I answer because my first thought is that, when the process took so long, where do I begin?

In the beginning of panic came the mistake of giving my surges of fear a wide space to live in and room service. I indulged my fears by coddling them. If I felt uneasy about getting on an elevator, then instead of pushing through the fear, I would walk up ten flights of steps to avoid the risk of panic. With every step I climbed, I ensured fear a stronger position of influence over me. Soon I avoided elevators completely. That's the pattern of fear's insidious grip. We give in; fear takes over. Fear demands control. Soon I was afraid to drive a car, then to ride in one. I slept inordinate hours to escape my scary world—besides, depression is one of panic's closest friends, along with a host of other tyrants (shame, hypochondria, anger, and guilt). By the time I had the audacity to begin reversing my patterns, I was housebound and often bed-bound.

My recovery began one morning when it came to me that my life was not only on hold but I was also running out of options for survival. So I went to my medical doctor and told him I didn't want one more pill. What I wanted was help to get well. So began my exodus from fear and the genesis of my healing. I stumbled around in my faith, learning how to trust the God who holds the wind in His fists.

I attended a mental health talk tank, where patients helped each other get well through identification (you are not the only one), discipline (life is too important to play games), and endorsement (you have value).

In the beginning, a child of fear came out of hiding, and a woman of faith emerged . . . God said, "And it was good."

Bits and Pieces

1. What stretches the canvas of your mind when you think about it?
2. Reflect on creation before humankind. What thoughts does it stir?
3. Which are you most prone to do—worry, fret, or fear? What's the difference between these?
4. What scary path have you walked? What was that like?
5. How have you indulged fear?
6. Do you have a sense of God's pleasure in you?

7. What do you need an exodus from?

8. What steps can you take today toward a new beginning?

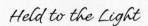

Held to the Light

In the beginning God created the heavens and the earth. (Genesis 1:1)

Cease from anger, and forsake wrath; do not fret—it only causes harm. (Psalm 37:8)

Therefore I say to you, do not worry about your life. (Luke 12:22a)

Do not fear, little flock, for it is your Father's good pleasure to give you the kingdom. (Luke 12:32)

But He said to them, "Why are you fearful, O you of little faith?" Then He arose and rebuked the winds and the sea, and there was a great calm. So the men marveled, saying, "Who can this be, that even the winds and the sea obey Him?" (Matthew 8:26–27)

CHAPTER 28

Oh, Happy Day

*As cold water to a weary soul, so is good news
from a far country.*

—PROVERBS 25:25

When our eldest son, Marty, headed to Guam with the air force, I was fixated on the telephone. We didn't have a cell phone at that time, so we had to stay close to home to ensure that we didn't miss hearing him tell us that he had landed safely and was settled. During that tedious interval of waiting, whenever the phone would ring, I would skyrocket across the room like one of those clowns shot out of a cannon. A couple of times I almost ruptured my spleen on the doorframe, trying to reach the phone first. I'm not sure why first mattered, but when the phone rang, it would launch me every time.

Soon my antics left me door-bruised and exhausted. Even my rest had turned fitful, causing my husband to flinch and duck in his sleep. And for good reason. Evidently after midnight, once I had fallen asleep, a latent gift for kickboxing surfaced. Who knew?

Finally Marty called. All was well on the other side of the world, and he was safely tucked away on the island. Whew. That night I slept like a farmer after harvest. Les slept on the couch. He was concerned I might be overcome with jubilation, fall asleep, and sling him across the room.

Good news can have a profound effect on us. We see that in the parable snapshot of the prodigal when the dad scans the horizon in search of his loved one. Remember when the father first saw his lost son from afar? His heart leapt with the realization that his boy was alive and coming home. What news! What relief!

The father's sudden surge of joy turned to adrenaline, and he tore off running toward his beloved boy. Faster and faster he ran until his wayward son, at last, was in his arms. The dad had dreamed and prayed for this reunion. He fell on the young man's neck and kissed him. His grateful tears streaked the ragged runaway with a daddy's relief. "And he arose and came to his father. But when he was still a great way off, his father saw him and had compassion, and ran and fell on his neck and kissed him" (Luke 15:20). (The story is found in Luke 15:11–32 if you care to read it in detail.)

I'm well acquainted with the good news of a prodigal's homecoming. I was one. When I returned home from my rebellious jaunt, my mom obviously had been steeping in the prodigal parable while I was gone. To my amazement she, too, had been scanning the horizon, and on my arrival, Mom came running out of the house, took me in her arms, and kissed me with many kisses. Her tears ran down my neck, washing me in a mother's relief. It was startling.

I was prepared for a beating, which is what she had promised all her children if we ever ran away. Quite honestly, beatings weren't Mom's style; she used more the throttle-you-with-words technique. Guilt was her weapon of choice.

Years later, I would look back and shudder at how frightening it must have been when I disappeared, and Mom had no idea where I was. When word came that I was in a far country, six hundred miles away, and that I was safe, I'm sure her relief was immeasurable. The good news removed any desire to guilt me—her sixteen-year-old, ragged runaway—into submission. Instead, she sincerely wanted to find a way to reconcile our differences.

Today, I can't watch reunions without getting teary. Probably some of those tears are still regret that I put my mom through so much.

Because I log many air miles with the Women of Faith tour, I regularly am witness to reunions, mostly servicemen returning home to their families. I'm the one standing off to the side, flicking tears.

I remember as a girl of twelve, my brother, Don, who was nine years older than me, returned from Germany after fulfilling his army stint. My mom started crying before he arrived, and by the time he pulled up outside and walked to the front door, she was shaking and sobbing. I found her reaction extreme . . . until I had children. Then it made perfect sense. Now that I have grandsons, if I don't see them for a week, when I do get my hands on them, I cover them with kisses as if I hadn't seen them in years. I am so grateful they indulge me!

My mom had many separations from those she loved, none harder than when my thirty-eight-year-old brother was killed in a car accident. On receiving the news, the jolt to Mom's body was immediate, as her back slipped out of place and a blood vessel burst in her eye. At the funeral home I had to lift her off my brother's casket several times. She was distraught.

The news from "the far country" that was like cold water to Mom's weary soul came from the apostle Paul's letters promising her that she would see Don again. Talk about good news. Mom comforted herself with that assurance until years later when she lost track of who she was and became a stranger even to herself. Eventually Mom left her used-up body and her spent mind for heaven's shore, our homeland, to meet her Savior . . . and her son.

I comfort myself now, knowing that one day this pilgrim—after I kneel and kiss the sweet feet of Jesus—will run as fast as my new legs will carry me and fall on my mom's neck and kiss her with many kisses.

Bits and Pieces

1. When have you been fixated on the phone? Who were you waiting to hear from?
2. When was your last teary reunion?
3. Look up the word *prodigal* in a dictionary and a thesaurus. When have you ever been a prodigal?
4. Who has greeted you with many kisses?
5. What is your weapon of choice when you want someone to shape up?
6. With whom do you need to reconcile? When will you do that?
7. When have you ever been inconsolable?
8. Why do you think *cold water* is used to describe good news in the proverb at the beginning of this chapter?

Held to the Light

Then he fell on his brother Benjamin's neck and wept, and Benjamin wept on his neck. Moreover he kissed all his brothers and wept over them, and after that his brothers talked with him. (Genesis 45:14–15)

And they told him, saying, "Joseph is still alive" . . . The spirit of Jacob their father revived. (Genesis 45:26a, 27b)

For here we have no continuing city but we seek one to come. (Hebrews 13:14)

These all died in faith, not having received the promises, but having seen them afar off were assured of them, embraced them and confessed that they were strangers and pilgrims on the earth. For those who say such things declare plainly that they seek a homeland. (Hebrews 11:13–14)

CHAPTER 29

It's the Nomad Life for Me

Keep your heart with all diligence, for out of it spring the issues of life.

—PROVERBS 4:23

I once lived in a house that had a sandbox in the backyard. My boyfriend Ricky and his brother lived next door. Ricky and I were three. I had a high-backed snow sled with my name on it. Down the street, Mr. Slotman grew carrots in his garden, and I thought they were quite wonderful. The Keglers lived across the street, and they had a boxer dog. The rooms in their house were dark. The lady on the corner was a widow with a high-pitched voice and a large facial mole. My brother was a paperboy. I went to school in a portable building. And then we moved.

Our new home was bigger and had a dining room full of large-flowered wallpaper. My room was lime green. The light switches were plastic, oval Roman heads. We had a fireplace and a porch. The garage was in the backyard. I received a spiffy two-wheeler. My dad drove an Oldsmobile. I had a Toni doll and a Tom Thumb typewriter. Cecelia was my friend. She lived next door. She was quiet and wore pretty dresses. We had a milk box by our side door. And then we moved.

Our next house was brick and had a rental unit upstairs. A nice dentist and his family lived there. The house had a scary cement basement with big sinks. You had to walk through the dining room to get to the bedrooms and kitchen. Sisters Elaine and Susan lived down the street; they had a children's kitchen in their basement. I took ballet lessons. The telephone was in the dining room. We found baby rabbits in our yard. They died. School was two blocks away. My brother joined the army. And then we moved.

We moved to a country setting. I attended an elementary school with glass halls, designed by a Japanese architect. Our house had a mural in the living room. The doors throughout were louvered. The kitchen was tiny. The wallpaper was from Paris. I slept in the recreation room on a couch bed. I had a bird named Tweetie. He died. I had a dog named Hunter. He disappeared. My parents almost bought me a donkey. Instead, we moved.

The new home was a small ranch in a neighborhood of kids my age. I was eleven. The paperboy liked me. I sold glittered candles. I had a hi-fi and a record by Patti Page. My mom gave birth to my sister. I was thirteen. We went on picnics. We had a green Coleman camping stove. I babysat for neighborhood children. I had an appendectomy. My niece was born in my bed. We moved.

This home looked like a suite on an ocean liner. I had a canopy bed. I won a call-in radio contest. The new paperboy liked me. The kitchen cupboards were knotty pine. We had caramel-colored dishes. I had a baby blue princess phone. I rode a school bus. I smoked. I ran away. I quit school. I got married. I moved.

Our first place was in the basement of a dilapidated mansion. It had roaches. And rats. I was afraid. We were poor. The floors were wavy. The old furniture smelled. We had no television. I spent most nights alone while Les was on the military base. I made a friend. Judy had food. She was smart. Les was sent to Germany. I moved.

And so began a circuitous new route as Les and I moved hither and yon for more than forty-seven years to date. During that time, we have lived in church camps, youth camps, a Boy

Scout reservation, a mobile home, a farmhouse, apartments, and houses galore.

Inside of all those moves are tucked joys and sorrows. Years of struggles. Years of babies. Years of jobs. We've laughed, cried, fought, and celebrated. And the journey goes on.

Through those years, I must confess, I lost track of my heart more than once. Sometimes I was so caught up in surviving, I wasn't consciously aware of how well I was living or how I was feeling. It was easy for me just to go from calamity to busyness to obligations to depression. Soon I just shoved my heart in a box and crated it around with the rest of my possessions.

It's easier to keep short accounts than to backtrack through the years, trying to reweave your life into some semblance of order. Trust me when I say that life accumulates. So rather than digging through the remnants, I recommend the counsel of Proverbs 4:23: "Keep your heart with all diligence, for out of it spring the issues of life." Making sure you're right with those in your life and not shoving your hurts and sorrows into some box keeps the sweet springs of life flowing. I highly recommend it.

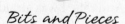

Bits and Pieces

1. Who was your first boyfriend?
2. How often did you move growing up?
3. How old were you when you got your first two-wheeler?
4. What pets did you have?
5. How many schools did you attend?
6. What did the first place you lived in look like?

7. What does it mean to keep short accounts?
8. Define *diligence*.

Held to the Light

Now the LORD had said to Abram: "Get out of your country, from your family and from your father's house, to a land that I will show you." (Genesis 12:1)

So Abram departed as the LORD had spoken to him, and Lot went with him. And Abram was seventy-five years old when he departed from Haran. (Genesis 12:4)

So God led the people around by way of the wilderness of the Red Sea. And the children of Israel went up in orderly ranks out of the land of Egypt. (Exodus 13:18)

The LORD our God spoke to us . . . saying, "You have dwelt long enough at this mountain. Turn and take your journey." (Deuteronomy 1: 6, 7a)

Now it came to pass in the days when the judges ruled, that there was a famine in the land. And a certain man of Bethlehem, Judah, went to dwell in the country of Moab, he and his wife and his two sons. (Ruth 1:1)

And Jesus said to him, "Foxes have holes and birds of the air have nests, but the Son of Man has nowhere to lay His head." (Matthew 8:20)

CHAPTER 30

Something Fishy

To know wisdom and instruction . . .

—PROVERBS 1:2*a*

My nutritionist told me that eating salmon would improve my brain function. Well, honey, I was all over that. I had been sputtering on two and a half cylinders, and I was in need of a mental lube job. I was way past my 100,000-mile oil change. Especially since my brain cells seemed to be thinning out at the same rate as my once-bushy hair.

But it wasn't long before I realized that daily fish leads to fins! I mean, how much salmon can one girl eat before she starts swimming in circles? Besides, I began attracting herds of cats, which isn't bad if one isn't allergic to them . . . but I am.

My mom was diagnosed with Alzheimer's and lived with my sister, Elizabeth, for the last seven years of her life. As the disease progressed, my mom regressed and was befuddled, which we anticipated.

The surprise came when Elizabeth noticed that if she fed Mom salmon, she mentally rallied. For brief moments, Mom would come back to us from the distant shores of uncertainty. When she had those times of clarity, my sister would call me. "Quick, talk to Mom; she just ate some salmon." And sure enough, for a few precious moments, Mom and I would have a loving chat . . . and then we would lose her again, as she would swim off to harbors we couldn't find.

What do you do to keep yourself mentally alert? Smart? Savvy? A lot of exercise propaganda—excuse me, I meant information—is out there that's impressive regarding the relationship between exercise and our brains. It makes sense—move your body, move your brain.

Several years into Mom's disease, Elizabeth had to incorporate a supplemental drink into Mom's diet because she wasn't eating well. At first she received it well, but after a time it evidently didn't suit her palate. Never a person to hold back her opinion, Mom let her displeasure be known. When the supplement was set before her, she made sport of it. She would pick up the can, and with a wicked overhand, she would spiral it at the kitchen wall, splattering the leftover contents to the uttermost parts of the room.

As you can imagine, Elizabeth initially was dismayed, but she soon decided, when the behavior continued, that the exercise value was worth the cleanup. So after that, when Mom would reach for the container, the family took cover. As the drink hit the wall, the family would step back out from their hiding places and applaud her physical dexterity. "That was a six, Grandma," Nick would call out, holding up his fingers. A smug grin would trickle across Mom's face as if she secretly knew the Olympics were within reach.

So far my approach to exercise is a bit tamer . . . sorta. When I'm really tied to my desk for days, I've learned to take little walk breaks and exercise moments. Walk breaks mean I toddle around the yard for five minutes. The time investment in exercise moments is dependent on the cleanup.

I like doing the exercise during which you hold your arms midchest and then straighten your right arm and pull it back to the chest and then the same on the left side. So far, I have shattered one lightbulb as I sent a lamp spinning in orbit; a statue of Moses, who now only holds five commandments; and a small glass clock that only *tock*s, no *tick*s. The salmon doesn't swim far from the stream.

Experts are now saying game playing improves mental agility. I tried some of those, but the ones with numbers lost me. Anything beyond my numerical age doesn't add up for me. Don't worry, no immediate need to press the button; I've always been that way. Maybe I should have tried some salmon before I tackled that tricky 9 times 7 stuff.

But I love crosswords and word challenges. I could play Scrabble all day. In fact, there was a time in my life when I did. I don't recommend that kind of time-eating involvement. That wouldn't be building brains; that would be called avoiding life.

If you want to combine exercise and games, Wii has made that possible. But I recommend starting slow. I spent a month in physical therapy because of overenthusiasm going down the ski hill. My gusto gauge is calibrated way too high.

Let's see . . . we can exercise, play mentally challenging games to help our gray matter percolate, and what was the other one? Oh, yes, that brings us full circle, back to brain food (must be time for my snack).

Don't worry, fish haters of the world. I'm not going to suggest you fish up your diet, but I am going to recommend we consider the words of Solomon in regard to our mental dexterity. In fact, he says it's the reason he wrote the book of Proverbs. Listen . . .

> . . . to know wisdom and instruction, to perceive the words of understanding, to receive the instruction of wisdom, justice, judgment, and equity; to give prudence to the simple, to the young man knowledge and discretion—a wise man will hear and increase learning, and a man of understanding will attain wise counsel. (Proverbs 1:2–5)

The more often we drop our line in God's Word, digesting and assimilating His truths, the more capable we are of living mentally astute lives. Don't misunderstand. I'm not suggesting that if we submerge our brains in Proverbs, we won't get Alzheimer's; my mom was an ardent fan of the Scriptures, and it didn't prevent her disease . . . but it sure helped her through.

Mom spoke of Jesus daily. She forgot her family's names—she called me "Nice Lady"—but the name of the Lord was on her lips to the end. How comforting to know they were on speaking terms, even through the darkest dip in the valley, as He took her hand and guided her home.

Nothing fishy about that.

Bits and Pieces

1. How are you and your brain getting along? Are you on speaking terms?
2. When do you feel smart?
3. Look up *savvy* in a thesaurus; list the alternative words. Would you describe yourself as savvy?
4. What kind of exercise regime are you on?
5. What kind of games do you play?
6. List five people you know who demonstrate mental agility.
7. How can you keep the name of the Lord on your lips?

Held to the Light

Jesus said to them, "Bring some of the fish which you have just caught." . . . [Soon] Jesus said to them, "Come and eat break-fast." (John 21:10, 12a)

And they said to Him, "We have here only five loaves and two fish." He said, "Bring them here to Me." Then He commanded the multitudes to sit down on the grass. And He took the five loaves and the two fish, and looking up to heaven, He blessed and broke and gave the loaves to the disciples; and the disciples gave to the multitudes. So they all ate and they were filled. (Matthew 14:17–20a)

"Please test your servants for ten days, and let them give us vegetables to eat and water to drink. Then let our appearance be examined before you." . . . So he consented with them in this matter, and tested them ten days. And at the end of ten days their features appeared better and fatter in flesh. (Daniel 1:12–15a)

How sweet are Your words to my taste, sweeter than honey to my mouth! (Psalm 119:103)

Your words were found, and I ate them, and Your word was to me the joy and rejoicing of my heart. (Jeremiah 15:16a)

. . . .

CHAPTER 31

A Window with a View

Wisdom is in the sight of him who has understanding.

—PROVERBS 17:24

I'm sitting in a hotel room in front of a window on the forty-sixth floor. I can see for miles. At least it seems like miles. I've never been good with spatial measurements. My dad would have called it "a mighty far piece." My Aunt Pearl would have said it was "way out yonder." The buildings below appear to be Monopoly pieces to set on Broadway or St. Charles Place while the traffic on the roads looks like ribbons and toy cars. One thing that stands out—because there are so many—are all the windows on the buildings. Who cleans those, anyway? I mean, some bird did something rude to the window I'm peering through, but who would climb up on the outside, forty-six floors up, to sponge it off? I'd pray for some rain and a puff of wind and call it done.

Speaking of windows, when I was a kid, my dad used to sing "(How Much Is) That Doggie in the Window?" Anybody remember that? He usually burst into this song when I was bugging him for a pet. Even though I didn't get my dog until I was grown and married, I still remember that teasing song with fondness. In fact, when I grew up and had my first baby, I bought a red and white toy dog. When you pulled its string, its eyes went back and forth while "(How Much Is) That Doggie" played. I guess we never get far from the things that connect us to our childhoods.

Along with letting in light and dark, windows connect us. Through a window you could oversee a child at play, a family member mowing the yard, or a pet chasing a squirrel. Windows also help us to observe . . . other stuff. I'm an appreciative shopper and love a well-tended showcase. So a couple of years ago, when my friend Carol and I took a train trip to Chicago to do some Christmas shopping, we squealed with delight at the window displays. They were right out of the 1940s, when designing a setting for fashion was a big, competitive business. Every window was treated like its own imaginative world. As Carol and I stood and marveled at the artistry, it began to snow, ever so lightly. Ah, perfect . . . like being in a shopping snow globe.

We've all heard the term *a window of opportunity*. It's a space of time during which we peek through the possibilities and make a choice. Will I or won't I? Like when I was invited to go to Africa. What a scary thrill. The scary part made me hesitate while the thrill made me lean in and wonder. That's the thing about windows—you can't see everything. In some cases that's good. Had I seen the tiny bush plane we would fly in to reach the Masai Mara, the dirt path we would land on, or the water buffalo stampede we would be caught in, I wouldn't have gone, and I would have missed having my world expanded about 360 degrees.

They say our eyes are a window to our souls. Now, don't ask me who says it, but I've learned a lot about folks from their eyes. Haven't you? If a child won't meet your eyes, there's a reason. Check the cookie jar. If a couple won't face each other eye to eye, there's a reason, probably many reasons. There's a sinister look that can be detected in eyes when someone is up to no good. And a tender look that literally floats in eyes when a vow is spoken or an infant is coddled. Have we not all experienced talking to someone who has that light-on-but-no-one-home look? Just a vacancy sign hanging in the window of his or her eyes.

Today, as I looked out from my forty-sixth-floor perch, I said to a friend, "Inside all those windows are people. And inside all those people are their stories."

What's yours?

Bits and Pieces

1. What's out your window?
2. Can you remember a "window" from your childhood?
3. What kind of things connect you to your past?
4. Do you have a favorite window view?
5. What window of opportunity do you regret missing?
6. What do you think your eyes communicate to those close to you?

Held to the Light

"Try me now in this," says the LORD *of hosts, "if I will not open for you the windows of heaven and pour out for you such blessing that there will not be room enough to receive it." (Malachi 3:10b)*

Now when Daniel knew that the writing was signed, he went home. And in his upper room, with his windows open toward Jerusalem, he knelt down on his knees three times that day, and prayed and gave thanks before his God, as was his custom since early days. (Daniel 6:10)

On that day all the fountains of the great deep were broken up, and the windows of heaven were opened. (Genesis 7:11b)

Then she let them down by a rope through the window, for her house was on the city wall. (Joshua 2:15a)

Blessed are your eyes for they see. (Matthew 13:16a)

The lamp of the body is the eye. If therefore your eye is good, your whole body will be full of light. (Matthew 6:22)

CHAPTER 32

Breath of Life

The great God who formed everything . . .

—PROVERBS 26:10*a*

If art lacks heart, it has no life. It can't breathe on you. But if you've ever examined a great work, you have marveled at the palpable beauty emanating from an inanimate object. For instance, a sculptor can chisel life out of a hunk of marble so beautiful that you can't bear to move away from the statue. You stand transfixed. You study the lines, muscles, hair, eyes, and that's when it happens . . . the breath of this masterpiece caresses your face. You know you will never forget this moment when first you met. The work takes up residence inside a niche of your memory.

I was in an art gallery in Georgetown when I saw the work of Frederick Hart for the first time. I was smitten. His sculpting was stunning. I couldn't seem to move away from it until I checked the price tags, and then my coin purse and I galloped toward the first stagecoach out of Dodge. His work was worth the price; it was just that the price was more worthy than my budget.

Later I visited the National Cathedral in Washington, DC, and saw Hart's *Ex Nihilo Tympanum*, which swirls over the door at the West Main entrance. I stood on the steps, head tipped back in a trance. I'm sure to arriving visitors I appeared to be misplaced yard art. My eyes couldn't hold all the beauty of Hart's depiction of creation, showing humankind's chaotic struggle.

On my return trip home from the airport, I stopped at the art fair going on in my hometown. As I meandered through the booths on the street, I entered one that was full of photographs. Casually flipping through a box of prints, I suddenly stopped as my heart flip-flopped. There before my eyes was a photo of Hart's Cathedral sculpture at a price I could afford. I was overjoyed. To this day it is one of my favorite pieces.

Think about it. This wasn't even the real deal, just a picture of Hart's work, like a cousin twice removed. How could I feel connected to something that was so removed from the original? Yet every time I see the print, I'm transported to the steps where I viewed the movement and beauty of the piece and first felt its breath. That's when I realized what great art has . . .

A pulse. Uh-huh. A pulse. No pulse, no life. No pulse, no breath.

Now, here's an assignment. Take your right hand and place it on your left inner wrist. What do you feel? A pulse! That makes us—get this—bona fide works of art.

If only we believed that. I tend to be almost manic in my evaluation of my worth. Thinking one moment too highly of myself because I'm sporting a new hairdo and my toenails are polished and the next feeling like a dime-store print left over from a garage sale. After I came to Christ as a young adult, my concept of my worth was given a whole new framework. But, I confess, it's my tendency to keep falling out of the frame.

I know Christ gave His life for me. I know He loves me. I know I'm forgiven because of Christ's sacrifice on the cross. Yet I still fall victim to my own thin humanity. It seems to be one of my besetting sins. I hear myself having to pray, "Forgive me for not being more tenderly respectful of me, for speaking so severely to myself."

Do you have a grumpy voice inside of you that denies the wonder of the way God created you? Do you judge yourself harshly if you make a mistake? Do you feel ashamed if you fail?

I do. Which is why I have to remind myself regularly of who I am in Christ. That I was created and that God said, "It was good." Because God always does good work. If you doubt that, gaze into the kaleidoscope of a starlit night; hold a newborn close to your heart; investigate the world inside a pond; stand near a waterfall; plant a garden; go on safari.

Even though I do a better job of extending grace to myself today, it's not without effort. I'm convinced some of the things we battle with will be a challenge for us until glory.

Appreciating your own value may come easily to you. Yet I know you battle something. I know that because of our stony condition. It takes a lifetime of sculpting to chip off our hard edges, to smooth out our uneven dispositions, and to chisel a heart of flesh within our marbleized interiors. And we can't do this work ourselves; it takes a Master Craftsman to breathe into us eternal life and to set a life-pulse within us.

God touched woman's heart and flowers grew
Fragrance rose up and songbirds flew.
God touched woman's heart the sky turned blue
Lilacs and roses cradled the dew.
God touched woman's heart and made her new
Sunflowers on tiptoes, glorious view.

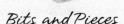

Bits and Pieces

1. Do you think art is important? Why or why not?
2. Who are your favorite artists?
3. What work of art leaves you breathless?
4. Do you personally feel like a work of art? Why or why not?
5. Are you more likely to frame yourself in a positive or negative light with others?
6. When was the last time the grumpy voice inside you tried to drag you down?
7. What did you do about it?
8. When was the last time you felt shame?
9. How would you describe who you are in Christ?
10. Write a poem that captures your heart.

Held to the Light

Before the mountains were brought forth, or ever You had formed the earth and the world, even from everlasting to everlasting, You are God. (Psalm 90:2)

Where were you when I laid the foundations of the earth? (Job 38:4a)

For you formed my inward parts; You covered me in my mother's womb. (Psalm 139:13)

I will praise You, for I am fearfully and wonderfully made; marvelous are Your works, and that my soul knows very well. (Psalm 139:14)

But as many as received Him, to them He gave the right to become children of God, to those who believe in His name. (John 1:12)

Be strong in the grace that is in Christ Jesus. (2 Timothy 2:1b)

. . . .

CHAPTER 33

Kaleidoscope Wonders

Is your head spinning with proverbs? Actually, that's a good thing. I hope you've stored a good many pieces of these truths in your heart so that, when life is tipsy and you turn to the light, you see clearly the patterns of God's plan.

Since this is the close of our musings on the book of Proverbs, I must share with you something I've learned about kaleidoscopes. It has made me pause and think once again of the magnitude of God. I hope it will you as well.

Inside a kaleidoscope are mirrors that reflect light, which gives us the color and images we see. When you have two mirrors inside a cylinder, you have a perfect, singular circle image. When you have four mirrors, you have a parade of images. But when you have three mirrors, the images are endless.

The number three is significant in Scripture and to our faith, especially in light of the Trinity—the Father, Son, and Holy Spirit. Our endless God. Isn't that great? We can never finish searching Him out. We will never "know it all." Yet I do believe God takes pleasure in helping us, His children, to view Him as many ways as we possibly can.

I especially love when God spins the kaleidoscope of nature for us. He allows us to see a smidgen of His glory in the heavens' expanse, the beauty of His strength in the rising sun, the generosity of His vigilant care in starlit nights, the power of His might in a raging storm, and His unending kindness in flower-graced meadows. That's just for starters; the story doesn't stop there. Creation, like its Creator, is endless from the layered story in a solitary seed to a waterfall, to a mountain, to a comet, to a galaxy. All the bits and pieces of the universe bear witness to God.

Life, too, is like a kaleidoscope. Our brokenness comprises life's kaleidoscopic shards, but when we turn it in God's direction, we see how He puts a whole new spin on our perspectives. God wastes nothing. He uses whatever touches our lives for divine purposes.

That in itself is a mystery. How can prejudice, injustice, or hatred be integrated into a holy plan?

Remember Old Testament Joseph? He was the brother who was sold off into slavery by his older brothers. Years later, when a severe famine struck the land, the brothers found themselves standing before their once disposable brother. Joseph was now second in command over Egypt and unexpectedly in charge of his siblings' destiny. The quaking brothers' hearts took a tumble when Joseph announced to them that what they did they meant for his harm, but God meant it for his good (Genesis 50:20).

In that spectacular perspective we who are believers take heart. God ultimately uses our past, secures our today, and holds our destiny. As chaotic as life is, as purposeless as some events seem, and as brief as our days are, God's plans are being fulfilled. And anything over which he pronounces, "And it is good," shall be exactly that.

Remember the inscriptions from the seventy-five-thousand-dollar kaleidoscope?

- Who could from thy outward case, half thy hidden beauties trace?
- Who from such exterior show, guess the gems within that glow!

- Emblem of the mind divine, cased within its mortal shrine.

Let's consider each line:

WHO COULD FROM THY OUTWARD CASE, HALF THY HIDDEN BEAUTIES TRACE?

I constantly have to remind myself that every person has a story. Every person has a purpose. Every person has talents and gifts. Every person deserves to be treated accordingly. It doesn't matter how impossible they act because hidden inside, possibly even from them, are God-given gifts and the flicker of eternity. I'm sure if we could put the bits and pieces of their fragmented lives inside a kaleidoscope and turn it to the light, we would be surprised at the beauty we would see. I think it would give us fresh compassion for even the most unsavory among us.

Aren't you surprised and encouraged by whom Christ took time to be with, how He conveyed His love and broke down stereotypes we so easily create? For instance, I'm not sure we would want to deal with the naked lunatic screaming in the cemetery. Or the prostitute dragged into Christ's presence fresh from her bed of lust. What about the beggars? I mean, beggars look so, well, unsavory.

I was with a few friends in a city far from home when we chose to walk four blocks to a restaurant. The four short blocks turned into six long blocks, and along the way we found ourselves standing among a group of homeless people. Uncertain as to our safety because of their disheveled appearance and threatening leers, we moved closer together and looked straight ahead. We arrived at the restaurant, ate, and when we were done, we called a cab.

I've reflected back on those people a number of times and wondered, *What would Jesus do*? I think we know.

WHO FROM SUCH EXTERIOR SHOW, GUESS THE GEMS WITHIN THAT GLOW!

Do you remember watching Jim Nabors in the role of Gomer Pyle, a gas station attendant, on *The Andy Griffith Show*? Jim was a big guy with such a childish voice, but then I heard him sing. I would never have guessed such an operatic voice came out of the same guy who went around squeaking, "Gol-ol-lee." I couldn't decide which voice was the most startling, Jim Nabors's or Gomer's.

We don't begin to know what gems God has placed within a living soul. Our potential surpasses our days on this earth. We can grow as long as there is breath in our bodies and an earnest will to learn.

Corrie ten Boom was not by today's beauty standards an attractive woman, yet she remains on my top list of *most dazzling* people I've met. The circle of gray braids on her head, her meager stature, her boxlike breadth, her thick Dutch accent all faded as the Spirit of God covered her as she spoke. I was held captive by her words, and she transported me into a concentration camp full of disease and death and then led me out to experience God's redemption. Had I passed Corrie on the street, I wouldn't have given her a second thought. How sad. How many of God's treasures have I missed because they came wrapped in brown paper and string?

EMBLEM OF THE MIND DIVINE, CASED WITHIN ITS MORTAL SHRINE.

I'm grateful that while we are cased in these earthly bodies for now, it will not always be so. One day our spirits will be eternally free, and we will trade in our mortality for immortality. Until then we have access to a "mind divine." That brings us full circle, back to Proverbs, this book of reminders, reproofs, and revelations. God's Word makes it possible to put on the mind of Christ, to think above our own thoughts, to understand beyond our own comprehension, and to reason life through a divine grid.

These three inscriptions, though meant to define the inside of a kaleidoscope, also are applicable to our own interior design. When our lives are placed on the tripod of God's love, we become a dimensional sight worth examining . . . again and again.

Dear Lord, infuse our faith with wonder. Dazzle us with Your ever-expanding presence. May we trace and retrace Your artistry and be astute enough to find You in every line. Fill our viewfinders with the sun, moon, and a cache of stars, that we might be mindful of Your sovereign care in our lives. Stir up Your Word within us. Continue to teach us the triune benefits of wisdom, understanding, and instruction. May You find us open to Your tutelage. Instill in us courage for the days ahead. Remind us often that we are Yours, and that no enemy or weapon can separate us from Your loving intentions. Amen.

About the Author

PATSY CLAIRMONT's quick wit and depth of biblical knowledge combine in a powerful pint-size package. She will help you laugh God's truths right into your heart. Patsy's mission to provide humor and hope for healing comes from her own struggles. God pulled together the emotionally fragmented pieces of her life, not only to free her but also to serve as a reminder that imperfect, *cracked* Christians are God's specialty.

A recovering agoraphobic, Patsy speaks to women from all walks of life: "Take a deep breath and pop a dark-chocolate bon-bon; we girls are in this together." As a result of her appearances at Women of Faith, which she has been a part of since its inception, Patsy addresses tens of thousands of women each month. She has also written more than twenty-four books, including *Catching Fireflies*, *All Cracked Up*, and *I Grew Up Little*, in addition to contributing to numerous Women of Faith multiauthor books.

Patsy loves a rainy day, a good book, and a deep cushioned chair. Given a day off, she shops, decorates, solves the world's problems with a friend over lunch, and hugs the stuffing out of her two grandsons, Justin and Noah. She also avoids numbers, celebrates words, and eats entirely too many chocolate chip cookies. Patsy and her husband of forty-seven years, Les, live in Michigan. They have two sons, Marty and Jason; a daughter-in-law, Danya; and a granddog, Cody, who jumps higher than Patsy is tall.

TELL ME EVERYTHING

By Marilyn Meberg, available 3/30/2010

With the wisdom of a counselor and the whit of a comedian, Marilyn Meberg untangles the issues in women's lives that hold them back from a vibrant relationship with Christ.

FRIENDSHIP FOR GROWN-UPS

By Lisa Whelchel, available 5/4/2010

Former *Facts of Life* star Lisa Whelchel shares her experiences of growing up without true friends, how she learned to find and develop them as an adult through God's grace, and how readers should actively pursue meaningful friendships as adults.

DOING LIFE DIFFERENTLY

By Luci Swindoll, available 5/4/2010

An inspiring account of Luci Swindoll's courageous life that teaches readers how to live savoring each moment, how to let go of regrets, and how to embrace dreams.

THOMAS NELSON

Since 1798